Praise for *Ripple*
and the Writing of William Powers

"Powers combines environmental writing in the vein of Thoreau with Zen, economics, warrior presence, and even a touch of dramas of the heart to present a holistic view of contemporary deliberate living. Readers interested in a simpler and more sustainable lifestyle will enjoy the flowing prose and concrete thoughts as they reflect on their own American dream."

—*Library Journal*

"Powerfully intimate and loving, these letters from a father to his daughter remind us what really matters on this earth—and one of those things is the connection we have to the beauty and meaning all around us in nature."

—**Bill McKibben**, author *Here Comes the Sun*

"Powers' eloquent memoir reveals the breadth of this conflict and the depth of one man's commitment to himself and his community."

—*Booklist*

"Powers speaks with the authority of one who has seen the ramifications of the flattening world . . . Students of environmental and globalization ethics will be just as interested in Mr. Powers' journey as the activist or layperson exploring how to motivate self and the world to move towards sustainability."

—*Foreword Reviews*

". . . offers precious insights into the ways that all individuals living in a fast-paced consumer culture might incorporate different ways of thinking about the natural world into their lives."

—**Publishers Weekly,** starred review (*Blue Clay People*)

"On rare occasions an author translates a transformative experience into a written account that is an inspirational call to the reader."

—*The Huffington Post*

"*RIPPLE* is a book filled with graceful, engaging prose about one of the most important issues of our time. In an era of great cynicism and ecological calamity, Bill Powers offers a different, more positive future, based on a turn away from our dominating view of nature as separate from ourselves. In a series of letters to his eldest daughter as she turns fifteen, Powers shares the wisdom of his remarkable life—the son of a priest and a nun who married; Peace Corps and other service in poverty-stricken countries; a decision to leave New York City for a small town in rural Bolivia, where he has lived for more than a decade, writing five books and teaching dozens of international students. Powers shows how separation from nature, especially in the era of ubiquitous smart phones and social media, leaves youth all over the world confused, depressed, deeply anxious and even suicidal. His empathy shines through in every page. Young people need this book. We all do."

—**John de Graaf**, filmmaker, activist, co-author of *Affluenza*

"*Ripple* is a wise and wonderful story, gentle but demanding of us that we embrace our close kinship to wild things. Its wisdom is something I suspect you will want to share in your family and outside."

—**Gus Speth**, former Dean, Yale School of the Environment

"We are glued to screens. We gulp bad news on our phones all day long. Thus we miss knowing ourselves as living beings on an infinitely vibrant planet. How do we find our way home? Through poignant letters to his daughter, Bill Powers tells of personal stories of his family and himself accommodating to the ideology of separation, and weaving these with teachings from history, biology, and regenerative practices. [*Ripple*] is truthful, and tender, as Powers searches for stories to help his beautiful fifteen-year-old daughter find meaning, purpose, and belonging in a life rooted in the rhythms of nature."

—**Vicki Robin**, author of *Your Money or Your Life*

Also by William Powers

Blue Clay People: Seasons on Africa's Fragile Edge

*Whispering in the Giant's Ear: A Frontline Chronicle
from Bolivia's War on Globalization*

*Twelve by Twelve: A One Room Cabin, Off the Grid
& Beyond the American Dream*

New Slow City: Living Simply in the World's Fastest City

*Dispatches from the Sweet Life: One Family, Five Acres,
and A Community's Quest to Reinvent the World*

Ripple

*An Intimate Exchange
of Urgency and Hope
Between
an Ecologist Dad
and His Daughter*

William Powers

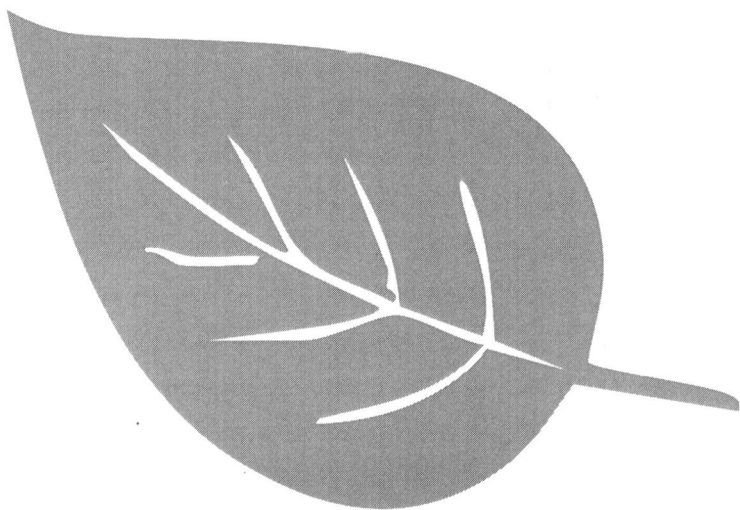

GREEN WRITERS PRESS | *Brattleboro, Vermont*

Ripple

An Intimate Exchange

of Urgency and Hope

Between

An Ecologist Dad

and His Daughter

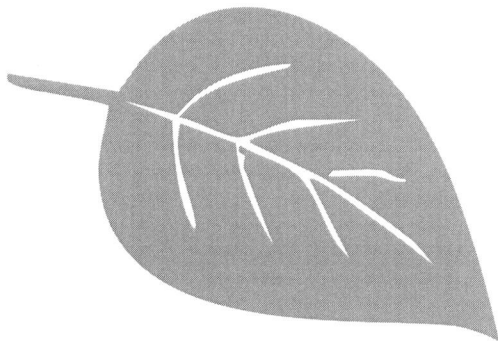

Green Writers Press is a Vermont-based publisher whose mission is to spread a message of hope and renewal through the words and images we publish. Throughout we will adhere to our commitment to preserving and protecting the natural resources of the earth. To that end, a percentage of our proceeds will be donated to environmental and social-activist groups. Green Writers Press gratefully acknowledges support from individual donors, friends, and readers to help support the environment and our publishing initiative.

GReen
wriTers
p r e s s

Giving Voice to Writers & Artists Who Will Make the World a Better Place
Green Writers Press | Brattleboro, Vermont
www.greenwriterspress.com

ISBN: 979-8-9914134-5-9

COVER IMAGE:
iStockphoto.com

COVER DESIGN:
Allison Pineault

INTERIOR DRAWINGS:
Amaya Powers

MIX
Paper | Supporting
responsible forestry
FSC
www.fsc.org
FSC® C103525

PRINTED AT KASE PRINTERS, ON FSC-CERTIFIED PAPER AND PRINTED WITH SOY-BASED INK, DEDICATED TO SOUND ENVIRONMENTAL PRACTICES AND MAKING ONGOING EFFORTS TO REDUCE OUR CARBON FOOTPRINT. WITH PAPER AS A CORE PART OF OUR BUSINESS, KASE IS COMMITTED TO IMPLEMENTING POLICIES THAT FACILITATE CONSERVATION AND SUSTAINABLE PRACTICES. KASE SOURCES PRINTING PAPERS FROM RESPONSIBLE MILLS AND DISTRIBUTORS THAT ARE CERTIFIED WITH AT LEAST ONE CERTIFICATION FROM AN INDEPENDENT THIRD PARTY VERIFICATION, SOURCED DIRECTLY FROM RESPONSIBLY MANAGED FORESTS. WE ALSO MAKE ONGOING EFFORTS TO REDUCE OUR CARBON FOOTPRINT, REUSE ENERGY AND RESOURCES, MINIMIZE WASTE DURING THE MANUFACTURING PROCESS, AND RECYCLE 100% OF SCRAPS, TRASH, CARTRIDGES, EQUIPMENT, AND SOLVENTS WHENEVER POSSIBLE. WE ARE A FAMILY-RUN BUSINESS, LOCATED IN HUDSON, NEW HAMPSHIRE.

All artwork by Amaya Powers

Contents

Prologue vii

I ↝ Aquifer

1. On the day you were born . . . *3*
2. Separation *7*
3. Biophilia Lost *15*

II ↝ Source

4. Initiation: *Hay Luz* *29*
5. But Can You Want What You Want? *39*
6. Future Zarahs *53*

III ↝ River

7. Re-tribe *65*
8. A Local Future? *75*
9. An American Transition Family *87*
10. Then you leave, and art begins *95*
11. The Reef *105*
12. This is Water *115*

IV ⇜ Estuary

13. Gaia's Seed *129*
14. A Wisp of Soul Carrying a Corpse *145*
15. *Amor Fati* *157*
16. Citadel *167*
17. The Knife *181*

V ⇜ Ocean

18. Freedom From Ambition *193*
19. Roar *211*
20. Rippling Further *223*
21. Living Bridge *235*
22. Seeds Dream Deep *249*

Ripple: Resources *257*

Prologue

Dear Amaya,

I scoured bookstores, libraries, and my own shelves to look for the right book for you now, at this tender moment in your life, as you turn fifteen and celebrate your Bolivian *quinceañera*. I was searching for what Kafka said a book should be: "an axe for the frozen sea within us."

But I couldn't find that axe. Instead, I found a river.

A river of philosophical and spiritual, scientific and ecological wisdom along which to navigate. I found Jeff VanderMeer, the "weird Thoreau," who uses speculative fiction to grapple with our relationship with the natural world. I found Ta-Nehisi Coates's *Between the World and Me*. We've already talked about how Coates speaks to his son through intimate letters reckoning with race. And I found Jenny Odell, who asks us to preserve our sacred inner silence in the attention economy.

Powerful as these and other books are, I found no place where all the ideas stream together in a way that might speak to you now. You and I have had deep talks lately, about the difficult things you are going through as you come of age, and how it relates to how we humans might once again *be nature*.

You're a mature, thoughtful person. One of your grandma's wise elder-friends calls you "an old soul." Remember the question we asked together the other day? It was something like: How can we journey beneath our conditioning in order to better connect with our instincts, heart, and *natural* mind . . . and not the mind a fast society of efficiency molds for us? This is the sort of inquiry we keep getting into, and no book I've found comprehensively speaks to it.

Then one day I began to realize something. I didn't want an axe. I wanted to flow, sharing ideas in relationship with you, and with readers.

When you were six, your first-grade teacher asked the class, "What's the biggest thing in the world?'"

A kid behind you piped up: "An airplane." "A mountain!" answered a second student. "A skyscraper," said a third.

At last, you raised your small hand and said: "My eye is the world's biggest thing."

Your teacher—telling me this story later—said that your response quieted the room. She asked you what you meant.

"An airplane, a mountain, a skyscraper," you replied. "They all fit into my eye. So my eye is the world's biggest thing."

The other night, Amaya, I came into your room and gave you a kiss as you slept. The tremendous love I felt for you as I watched you sleep blended with a bit of apprehension because you're about to come of age in a world of crisis. I felt—as millions of other parents do—baffled by how to bring up our children real. It may sound anachronistic, but, as you turn fifteen, I want to be human with you, our bones and plasma evolving with the patience of a river course.

In these first glorious fifteen years of your life, I've learned as much from you as you have from me. As you commemorate your *quinceañera*, what could possibly carry you further? I yearn to reach out with what I can offer: a reminder of the preciousness of your deepest humanity and inner wisdom, the world's biggest thing.

I

Aquifer

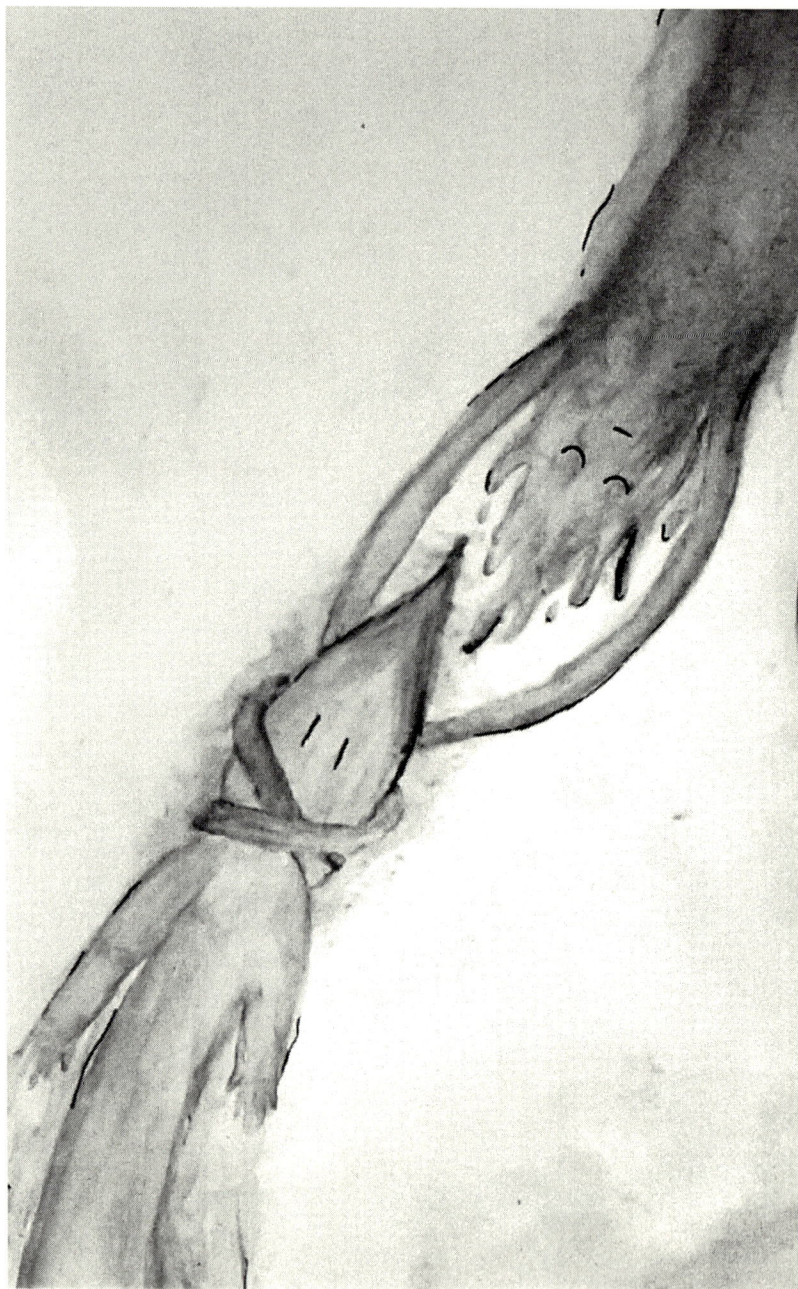

One

On the day you were born, could you taste birdsong?

Dear Amaya,

On the day you were born, I looked into your liquid eyes. You squirmed in my arms in confusion over the newness of air. You were still water.

As adults, the percentage of our bodies that is water drops to half, but as newborns our bodies are 95 percent water. Initially aquatic, we float for moons in salty embryonic fluid before bursting from darkness into a strange dry light, our sodden bones, plasma, and eyes still marine.

On your first day, your eyes *were* love. They were, to this dad, the world's biggest things. When you stopped bawling for a moment and squinted up at me for the first time, I felt the inexplicably primal sensation of an animal parent gazing at his first born. But your quiet did not last. You took in the strange land-giant holding you, then wailed again, tears streaming onto your already wet body. I passed you back to your mother, her face filled with wonder, joy, and relief that you'd completed the passage.

In a rare and puzzling condition called synesthesia, a person's senses, in effect, cross. Swiss musician Elizabeth Sulston, for example, hears pleasant chords as the taste of sweet cream, and tastes dissonant, grating chords as bitter. Sulston was the first known case mixing sound and taste. Much more common is the blurring of sound and sight where, for example, the sound of a birdcall "looks blue." Scientists believe the condition originates in the limbic system, a mysterious region of the brain associated with behavior and emotion. Studies on infants suggest that we all start out as synesthetes, but, after birth, neural circuits somehow become pruned and we lose this ability. An ancient biology, now nearly lost to us.

On the day you were born, could you taste birdsong? Were you absorbed within the life force as breastmilk rippled through you like sunlight? Certainly, a human infant treading embryonic water inside the womb, or kicking the air outside the womb, senses itself as no less Nature than a dandelion or a mountain lion.

Do you remember?

"Sometimes all I can think about is that nothing matters, Daddy." This is what you said to me recently, age almost fifteen. Then you added: "You live and you die and that's it."

Before you spoke, I knew you felt troubled. Your eyes were clouded as we sat, side by side, on the bank of our favorite river in Bolivia. I sensed you wanted to tell me something important but didn't know how, and I didn't want to pressure you to talk, so I waited. I listened to the river.

As I listened, the city's discordant hum jangled my senses—its vibrations of engines and horns—but this began to dissipate. Its frenzied noise had been dissolving from within me during the drive to this riverbank from Santa Cruz, where I picked you up from your mom's house. A bush taxi carried us along a potholed highway that rose into the Andean foothills, into yellow *carnival* trees and giant ferns, into a reprieve from traffic and screens. This was the road to Samaipata, the hill town where we have spent most of our time together over your last fifteen years. This time, however, we arrived at the end of a dirt road to meet your stepmom, Melissa, and your sister, Clea, and then bushwhacked together to a riverside campsite.

As I waited for you to speak, a river eddy—gleaming like steel—flashed and reminded me of a knife I had in a former life, back when you were little. For a moment, I could see its cold, sinuous blade and feel the heft of its ironwood handle in my hand. You and I were apart during that time. Separated.

I was in my native New York City so I could work and send remittances back to your mother in Bolivia. I missed you and felt guilty I was not able to kiss you every night before bed. My face often showed the same angst now on yours as I attempted to live sanely in the city. More than once I considered the elegance of the blade as I thought: *Nothing matters. You live and you die and that's it.*

As the light faded that day with you by the river, your words were with me as Melissa built a small campfire beside the river. You and Clea roasted marshmallows and then lay down by the fire, exhausted, your heads in my lap. Parrots roosting above, we all gazed into the flames, and I gave you each a head rub, awed by the two beautiful mammals nuzzling into me.

Instead of feeling nested in place and community, how is it that we humans at times sense ourselves as disjointed pieces of a world where *you live and die and that's it?* Your troubling words connect to what you and your teenage friends have told me: that you often feel like disconnected fragments within a climate-altered, pre-chipped, and otherwise-Separated world. It makes me wonder.

As I massaged your temples by that campfire, a surprise blaze of molten orange shot through the graying light. The final sunset colors arrived unexpected and intense. And with that spectacular blaze came a clear insight.

I decided to write these letters to you, as a gift for your fifteenth birthday. Until that moment, I'd only been considering the letters, but now I knew. My hope was to reconnect—together—to the beautiful, precious life force which is our very essence. More than that, I'd invite you into this vital conversation, to share as much of an exchange as feels authentic to you.

I gazed over the moonlit Piray River. A breeze snatched a leaf from its branch, causing the leaf to loop skyward, then tumble and tumble and tumble, somersaulting to the river's moon-glistened surface.

The leaf floated around a bend, drifting downriver through the shadows toward an estuary to someday dissolve into ocean. I imagined a parallel journey for you and me, one that begins with a mystery at once tiny and immeasurable: a somersaulting leaf kisses water. *Ripple.*

Two

Separation

Something was already around you in the hospital, on the day you were born. Something that existed long before you did. Something which subtly infuses all of us throughout our childhoods. *A story.*

You closed your beautiful eyes. As you slept beside your sleeping mother on the hospital bed, the sound of the TV in the lobby wafted in: advertisements for cell phones and soft drinks. Snack wrappers filled the trash basket in the corner. Corporate-branded medications filled the shelves. A doctor came in, but he didn't look at you. Peering instead into a laptop, he announced: "Her numbers are perfect." Out the window, trucks and taxis raced, spewing smoke into the sky.

I am thankful both for that doctor and for the machines and medicines that assisted you at your birth. But it's with hazard that I look no further than how that hospital benefits you and me. Let's look a bit beyond your hospital room to the world taking shape around you on the day you were born. Goldman Sachs, around that time, announced that "digitizing everyday objects will establish networks between machines, humans, and the internet," thereby creating *"new ecosystems* to enable higher profitability." The word ecosystem, long referring to the marvelous natural world, was becoming the world of humans-and-machines.

And when you were a toddler, Google's Ray Kurzweil, in a similar way, informed us that our food will soon come from "AI-controlled vertical buildings" and include "in-vitro cloned meat."

This gets me thinking of one of my acquaintances, who recently quit an executive job at Google. When asked why he resigned, he said it was because of the troubling results of a new study of American twelve-year-olds. The survey asked: "If you had to give up one of these three things, which would it be? Your phone, your internet connection, or your sense of taste." Seventy-two percent responded that they'd give up their sense of taste.

As small kids, those same twelve-year-olds may have felt—like you articulated in first grade—that their eye was the world's biggest thing, that their mammal bodies and minds were at once undivided from the rest of creation and at the same time potent. What led them to the point where they'd agree to swap a core sensorial experience for a screen?

On the day you were born, beneath the specific stage and props of your hospital birthplace—and beneath the visions and actions of the corporations shaping your external world—a *narrative of disconnection* already surrounded you.

This is the Story of Separation, where we privilege our species with superiority. Deafness to the song of the world that surrounds and sings within all creatures. Human supremacy. Eight million *different* species grace this planet, and we're driving so many of them into extinction through an economic growth model that privileges only humans.

Try asking yourself: "If I had to give up either my smart phone and all internet connectivity or my sense of taste and smell, which would it be?"

Allow yourself some space to consider this question deeply. What might your answer suggest about who you are today? . . . about the kind of future you desire for your kids and grandkids?

Daddy,

I did this exercise with a few friends and OMG. I think they're too embarrassed to admit they'd chose Wi-Fi.

If I had the chance—without having to suffer the consequences of complete and total isolation from the modern world :)—I would give up my phone immediately.

I've doom-scrolled way too many times. Doom is a fantastic way to describe it, a sort of mind trap of reading negative news stories for quick fixes that then make you drop into depression. I've uninstalled or disabled a lot of apps, but I find myself crawling back to them. Am I trying to run away from my own thoughts?

I've seen too many peers who have never tasted life without screens. You can feel it at times in class or during conversation that our minds are unused to the physical world. Without the restraint of social norms the internet is cruel. And since I'm a "digital native," it feels like my native place is frozen.

That's part of what I was saying to you down at the river. But I'm still trying to figure out why all of this makes me feel that way. And what to do about it. It's hard to step away from what makes you feel connected.

While harvesting pomegranates in our Samaipata orchard today, I recalled our mutual love of crafting or recalling anagrams. Funny ones like: the cockroach > *Cook, catch her!* And Butterfly > *Flutter by.*

But the latest anagram you shared with me had a more sophisticated tone. "Rearrange the letters in 'the meaning of life,'" you said, with a wry smile, "and out comes: *'The fine game of nil.'*"

We laughed together at this, and I continue to appreciate your growing up and playing around with words and irony. At the same time, it got me missing the days of more innocent anagrams. Your recent anagram, like the words you spoke to me by the river, suggests how we are suffused with a Separated meaning of life that—at its hollow core—is a fine game of nihilism.

Most of us don't usually realize that we exist within an order that is imagined. Yet all of us live, to one extent or another, within an invented story of the people, The Story of Separation. In a thumbnail version, it goes something like this:

Long ago, humans lived in groups that would max out at about a hundred before splitting into an offshoot community. This is still the way of other primates, who live in small communities nothing like today's mass-human societies of millions.

Around seventy thousand years ago, human brains evolved a unique ability: to imagine ourselves as part of something far larger than what we could see and touch. It's known as the Cognitive Revolution, and it gave humans the unique ability to connect with many, many thousands of others, far beyond the people we could actually see, through shared narratives. We're talking about narratives like "We are all of such and such a 'nation'" or "We share the common belief in a 'religion'" or "We all share a particular grand ideology, like 'fascism' or 'communism.'" No other species has this ability to imagine themselves as groupings of millions, or even billions, through the power of story.

Thus, we created ever larger societies bonded not by flesh-and-blood connections but rather by narratives. Narratives, invented by us.

This ability to live in ever-larger groups stitched together by stories led to the Agricultural Revolution where we domesticated animals, grew our own food, and began to build cities and develop arts and culture.

Through the centuries, our superior brains helped us advance as a species. Sure, we weathered setbacks of wars, plagues, and otherwise-Dark Ages, but our ingenuity always overcame such holdups. For example, we eliminated the threat of dangerous beasts, reducing their populations to cosmetic levels or domesticating them into our service. And we've incrementally reduced social ills, like discrimination of all types.

We are still imperfect, but "progress" continues to perfect us. We harness the power of billions of people connected by cooperating toward projects which could extend our lives toward immortality. In that noble quest, we'll harness the resources of forests, ocean floors, and even the moon and other planets. We will continuously improve ourselves through molecular modification, the fusion of robotics into our bodies, and whatever else we think up next.

The full Story of Separation is long and nuanced. It's enough for now to begin to reflect on how, and why, this narrative has become normalized. As you come into high school as your path is tracked more directly into college entrance, there's likely a subconscious version of this Story that goes something like: "Well, yeah, humans have obviously evolved as superior to other species—that's why we have the smart phones and skyscrapers and space stations. My role is to forge a career that helps advance progress and make the world a better place."

This sounds logical. But I wonder: is it logical mostly to our brains, which have been conditioned since birth into Separation? Could there be a more natural logic—a kind of innate wisdom—concealed beneath?

Forgive me, and I know this will feel like you're sitting in my classroom, but as a professor the habit is hard to break, LOL. (Okay, no more internet slang from this dad. I promise.)

One way to consider these "meta" questions is to pretend for a moment that you are an outsider to our species, an extra-terrestrial who just arrived to Earth. From that vantage point, consider four key things about the Story of Separation:

First, this Story is speciesist. In other words, it tells a guiding story that reduces "reality" to the lens of a single species' brain, when millions of distinct species currently inhabit our planet. What might the Story of dolphins be? While it's true that humans come out superior when assessed on a scale of human intelligence, if we look at sonar capacity, navigational ability, dexterity, olfactory ability, or even empathy, we are not a superior species.

Second, this narrative is imagined. Objective phenomena like rocks, trees, and water are real, but phenomena like free markets, liberal democracy, or even the environment—when abstracted as a separate "thing" that exists outside of ourselves—occur only in our imaginations. Nowhere else. Yet we believe such stories are real, and then act them out into external forms because we've been thoroughly educated into them.

From the first moments you've experienced the world—through language, television, and simply looking out the city bus window—you've been constantly reminded of the principles of the imagined order, which are incorporated into *anything* and *everything*. They are incorporated into films, fairy tales, paintings, songs, etiquette, political propaganda, and architecture.

During the pandemic, we didn't have to use our imaginations all that much to feel like extraterrestrial outsiders observing an imagined social order: Covid did that work for us. Our daily routines of work, school, and family life—even of how we dress—were altered. Global economic, health, transportation, and food production systems that once functioned in the background for many of us were destabilized or changed, forcing into our daily awareness anxieties about, for example, whether there would be enough toilet paper, flour, or milk at the local store.

Third, in the Story of Separation, our "species" is not based on biology, but rather sociology. Biologically, species are organisms similar enough to mate and create fertile offspring. But when we think about humanity, who is most fully human? Consider how hundreds of millions of poor and indigenous people are dehumanized in our thoughts, actions, and non-actions. A rural Sierra Leonean woman, like the diamond-rich earth below her feet, is valued only in terms of her contribution to Progress. If she, and the "natural resources" she inhabits, fail to contribute to economic growth, they are ignored. If they obstruct it, they are to be converted to Progress or eliminated. Ecofeminists like Vandana Shiva have made this connection between the marginalization and abuse of women and the marginalization and abuse of Mother Earth.

Whiteness—as you and I have talked about—is how humans have created the "white race." This includes white culture and a system of advantages given to white people through government policies and also through the way decisions are made in corporations, schools, and the courts. Through the perspective of Separation, Whiteness is another facet of the imagined order. I am white, and you, *hija*—daughter—are half-white, but through awareness of it as part of a Separated metafiction, we begin to dissolve it. It's true that we continue to reap the privileges of our skin color. But through our family process of decolonization, we've been working to face and transform it. (We'll talk more about that downriver.)

Fourth—and this is perhaps the hardest to grasp—the imagined order *shapes each of our inner worlds.* Your very desires are hacked. Most people do not wish to accept that the order governing their lives is imaginary, but, in fact, every person is born into a preexisting imagined order. His or her desires are shaped from birth by its dominant myths, and our personal wishes thereby become Separation's most important defenses.

And this is where it gets very, very tricky: the depth and complexity with which the imagined order has invaded our inner space means we have to be wary—and probe with great attention—where our true "inner voice" is coming from. And that's exactly the deeper sort of preparation we're about to explore.

Try this for a few moments: Gaze up from this book and into the distance. Focus on something; a swaying tree, a cloud, maybe a nearby house seen through the window. Do not label it in any way. Can you allow it *to be* without mental interpretations?

If you touch this state of "no-mind" even for a moment you've made a leap toward piercing the illusion of the Sapiens imagined order. You're perceiving the world from your deeper identity as nature itself. This is what Buddhists call "the observer presence."

Three

Biophilia Lost

Dear *Hija,*

When you were eight years old, you saw a few bigger kids chucking rocks at a wild three-toed sloth in the woods adjacent to your Bolivian school grounds. You ran over and stood between them and the sloths. Then you gathered three of your fellow third graders and convinced the principal to let your small tribe go around to all grades, including the high school, to explain to your classmates the importance of treating animals with care and respect. How passionately you urged kindness toward animals!

That feeling you experienced as a child is what you and I have been talking about: *biophilia*, a human's natural love for the web of life of which we are strands. From our DNA on up, we're intrinsically *inter*connected within ecosystems, so we feel good when we belong to nature. On the flip side, we do not feel good when we are disconnected from the rest of life.

The word biophilia may sound a bit clinical, even cold. The fact that we need to use a word like this for the innate connection to our own bodies and the rest of life seems like further evidence of our species' Separation.

Author David Foster Wallace shared a parable in his 2005 Kenyon College commencement address: *There are these two young fish swimming along, and they happen to meet an older fish swimming the other way. The older fish nods at them and says: "Morning, boys, how's the water?" And the two young fish swim on for a bit, and then eventually one of them looks over at the other and goes: "What the hell is water?"*

Foster Wallace then went on to say, "The immediate point of the fish story is that the most obvious, ubiquitous, important realities are often the ones that are the hardest to see and talk about." He cautions, however, that such realities "are of life-or-death importance."

What is it that "the fish"—we ourselves—don't see? Is it the life force, or the energy that animates the world, including our minds and bodies? Maybe we don't see it because we're lost in our repetitive thoughts, in our overscheduled and screen-laden lives. Cocooned, you might say, in individual and collective ego, in concepts like *progress* and *busyness* and *connectivity*.

To reconnect with biophilia, you might try the following visualization:

> Put down this letter, close your eyes, and picture a time when you felt really good. What were you doing and where? Were you alone or with others? What were the sounds and scents around you?
>
> Take a minute or so right now and go to that place, whatever it is for you.

I don't know what you've just imagined. But I have some idea about what your happy place might be. Over the years, I've given this visualization to dozens of groups in college classes and specialized workshops. I ask the audience if anyone wants to share what they pictured. Hands always shoot up, and, in hundreds of responses, not once did a person mention anything overly complicated, technology connected, or expensive. While half-immersed in the scene of their imagination, people describe places that are simple and usually nature connected. For example: "Running in the woods of my childhood." "Cooking a meal with a few close friends." "Walking a moonlit beach." For me, it's often memories of our shared times near the river or in the garden. What effervesces to the surface in that safe space *is* biophilia, *is* the love of life.

Why, then, does our contemporary world condition us to desire—and then manufacture for us—so much that is the opposite of our core happiness?

When you defended those three-toed sloths on your school grounds, some of the older kids mocked you. I can relate. When I was an eighth grader, I, too, was taunted for something similar.

It was a spring morning between classes, and I'd stopped to smell a dogwood flower on a tree behind the school. I didn't hear some kids sneaking up behind me. After hours of chalk-dust drudgery, I enjoyed the buttery scent. Suddenly, I felt myself shoved into the branches. "What are you, a freakin' tree hugger?" yelled a bigger student, a grade above.

There was snickering behind him, as others gathered. *Tree hugger* was one of the worst 1980s Long Island schoolyard insults, partly because environmentalists were seen by many students' parents as economic saboteurs. This was a myth pushed in part by corporations who didn't want to pay for the damage they caused to common water, air, and soil.

The older kid picked up a dogwood flower from the ground. "Sniff it *again*," he said, then pulled me into a chokehold, stuffed the flower against my nose and closed eyes, and then packed it in my mouth to the point where I couldn't breathe.

Another of the kids kicked me in the groin. The pain seared. They flung me to the ground and delivered several bruising kicks to the ribs. "Tree hugger," someone hissed before they dashed away.

I felt embarrassed for being weak, and for the rest of that day I loathed those kids. But on reflection now I wonder: doesn't it make sense? It's logical: if you internalize the Story of Separation, you'll injure sloths, and humans, too.

But it gets more nuanced because, as a kid on Long Island, I was Separated as well. I sensed this even if I couldn't name it yet.

No, I wasn't beating up others for infractions to the Story, but in many ways, I was similar to those kids: I shopped at the mall, aspired to have my own car, and watched TV each day. I attended the same public high school they did, a school where one teacher would regularly remind our "honors" class: "Your life comes down to one thing, kids—the bumper sticker on the back of your parents' car."

We knew this dark irony to be pressure toward the next label we could attach to ourselves, like Binghamton, Vassar, and Cornell. We were mostly naive to the coded meaning. The deeper message of the bumper sticker: PROGRESS.

It's been said that environmentalism is the first social movement in history where the enemy is ourselves. In other words, we can't just blame governments or corporations because *our* consumption stokes climate chaos and shoves other species—and our own, perhaps—toward extinction. But in the aquifers there are no enemies. It wasn't that teacher's fault for pushing bumper stickers, nor those kids' fault for pushing me, nor my own fault for pushing myself toward ambitions. That all flowed into your dad's hospital room, too, on the day he was born.

Humanity's extraction-from-habitat goes back millennia, but it hit overdrive during the Second Industrial Revolution in the 1880s as industry broke from the localized, small-factory, and guild system and began assembly-line mass production which tamed humans into becoming replicable labor units in vast production systems.

Then it hit hyperdrive during the Information Revolution in the 1980s, and then during the subsequent "Nano" Revolution happening now, where this productivity is slipping into our organic tissues. Powering such momentous shifts were, and are, ordinary people. People like your own Irish great-grandparents in New York City.

My dad's parents arrived from Ireland to urban East Coast America in the 1920s. Without much education, they worked hard at whatever jobs they could find: your great-grandma as a domestic worker and your great-grandpa selling tokens for the PATH train between Manhattan and New Jersey. They met and began to fall in love on the boat *back* to Ireland. (After a number of years in the US, they were both going back for a visit.) Upon their return to New York, they married and started a family. That was Pop's final trip to the old country—"An Irish dog will never bark at me again" is how he put it. He'd discovered what would be his lifelong home.

Compared to their parents' life in hardship-struck Europe, US capitalism delivered them previously unimaginable luxuries. Sure, your great-grandparents were resistant to the work-and-spend cycle, given the frugality and do-it-yourself ethic of their rural upbringing. But they nevertheless began to absorb advertising, first through radio and print, then television, and at all times through a cultural context pushing more-is-better. Such immigrant Americans joined nearly everyone else in purchasing and carrying into their living rooms the electronics which taught them how to be "modern" through radio dramas and TV series portraying households with the same consumer goods pushed in the ads. The firms producing this "new media" were large corporations, and the quick-changing, planned-obsolescence product culture they engineered convinced millions to toss out last year's fashions for new-and-improved ones.

One morning in the late 1930s, per our family's lore, a pair of uniformed Con Edison technicians knocked on your great-grandpa's working-class row house door in Queens and told him there was a problem. They wanted to put an electric streetlight up in front of your great-grandparents' house, they explained, but there was a tremendous oak tree growing there.

They asked him if they could cut it down. Otherwise, they'd have to put the light farther down the block.

He is said to have pondered it, looking up into the branches of that century-old oak. Then he finally pronounced, in trademark brevity: "I'd rather have a light than a tree."

A crew came later that day and felled the giant. And in the oak tree's place they raised a marvelous pillar of mined steel, crowned with electric *light*. The status of a huge metal mast manufactured in an industrial plant and bringing sunlight into darkness. Behold!

I can relate. He wanted to be part of a civilization offering the miracle of Progress to his family. Burn the coal of ancient oceans a hundred miles away, shoot its invisible juice into Queens, and illuminate his own stoop at public expense? This was the original no-brainer. We may be more aware today that such a tree provides shade, secretes oxygen, sequesters dangerous atmospheric carbon, and harbors urban wildlife, so we are more hesitant to cut it down. Yet we still make daily choices which, in the name of comfort, further extract our species from its broader body of nature.

I often think of the carbon burned when I fly, for example, yet I still do it. Invited to give campus lectures on Deep Ecology in Michigan, I acted from Deep Separation and cooked fossil fuels aplenty getting the two us there from Bolivia. Though I may have offset our trip's carbon by purchasing tree-planting credits—and I also justified the trip as facilitating a chance for you to visit your US family—none of this offsets the depth of a speciesist ethic that penetrates so much of what we tell ourselves we absolutely must do.

It reminds me of a joke from comedian George Carlin: "I don't believe there's any problem in this country, no matter how tough it is, that Americans, when they roll up their sleeves . . . can't completely ignore." Not just Americans, of course, but "modern" people everywhere have convenient blind spots built into the *You consume and you die, and that's it* story undergirding our behaviors.

A generation passed. Your grandparents—my mom and dad—must have sensed there was something awry with this underlying ethic. Hearing spiritual callings when they were teenagers like you are now, they diverted from the traditional college-and-profession track of their siblings and entered Catholic religious life.

Your Pop became a priest and your Giggi, a nun. Before they even knew each other they took parallel paths, committing to voluntary poverty and spending nearly fifteen years inside America . . . but outside mainstream Separation. Your grandparents explored progressive "liberation theology" as they worked on behalf of New York City's marginalized, and they also rose at five o'clock each morning to pray and contemplate.

Thus, they were molded not as individual profit-maximizers pursuing Progress, but rather as voluntary-simplifiers nested in spiritual collectives.

Their original vows were to be replaced by marriage vows. Though still faithful, they both got swept up in a 1960s countercultural zeitgeist. Your grandparents had long pressured, alongside thousands of other priests and nuns, the Church patriarchy to permit women priests and also allow priests to marry, but, ultimately, this movement sputtered. So your grandparents left their orders in order to start a family.

With only three thousand dollars and no assets, Giggi and Pop became teachers able to afford a small prefab house in a working-class, mid-Island subdivision. Along came my sister, your *tía* Amy, and me, into a countercultural nuclear family living on the edge of a beautiful suburban forest. They grew a productive strawberry patch, placed a statue of animal-loving St. Francis at its center, and taught us to appreciate the migrations of great white egrets. Less conditioned into work-and-spend capitalism than most of the neighborhood kids' parents, our family evolved within a sort of Catholic biophilia.

At that time—the early 1970s—parts of Long Island still thrummed and sang, splashed and whooshed. Your *tía* Amy and I would follow your Giggi through the woods around our home, fragrant with pine, peat, and moss. We spent hours in that forest, every so often playing the game I Spy. "I spy something fluffy," Mom might say, and my sister and I would stop to scan the living woods. *Does she mean the dandelion seed head? That cloud?* And, at last: *Oh!*, one of us would shout, spying bramble-snagged rabbit fur.

Sometimes we'd search our woods for eastern box turtles, their bulges barely apparent beneath a carpet of brown leaves. My sister or I would run over and push away the leaves, usually finding a rock or a log, but other times we'd spy flecks of rusty orange, then feel the surprise of a ridged tortoise shell.

We'd carry the box turtle home to play with it for hours before releasing it back into the forest. I felt a seamlessness between myself and the box-turtle-strewn woods around us.

Back then Long Island's population was half what it is now, its per capita consumption a third of today's, and climate-changing gasses still hovered at wieldy levels, so that the landscape in which we lived was less plundered. As a kid in nature, I understood, as humans do when we're young and still only mildly socialized, that box turtles are beautiful. I loved their ridged shells, so gratifying to touch, and the way they devoured strawberries from my fingers. For hours I'd watch the box turtles' patient, agile motions, similar to how your sister does today in Samaipata with our yellow-footed turtles, Shelby and Sheldon.

My sister and I *lived* biophilia as we sprinted through our oak forest beside a winded mother, our eyes spying turtles that dwelled inside the same breathing, interconnected organism that we did: that forest, the soil, the web of life.

So, you'll understand why the breach startled me.

It began with a rumble. Then came the sight of a yellow machine. Trees crashing, an engine roaring, the reek of diesel. Wheels flattening the oak-leaf bulges. *Steel crunching box turtles' shells.*

Tears flooded my cheeks, and Mom tried to hold me back not just from that machine coming toward us, but also from something else: the knowledge that our landscape was not an interconnected oaks-air-humans-turtles web. Rather, it *belonged to bipeds*, in this case to the "legal owners" (an imagined concept) of the new "subdivision" (also imagined) about to go up next to ours.

As Giggi held me back from attempting to stop the machine from killing trees and box turtles, I wonder if she intuited how tough it was going to be to raise her kiddos as St. Francis-style nature-lovers when something very powerful encircled our family.

Indeed, that something *inhabited* our family. It pushed through our suburban walls and seeped up into our wells from the Aquifer. Gradually—and sometimes all at once—that *something* flattened intrusions like box turtles and liberation theology.

Sunlight glared off the yellow machine as it roared toward us, knocking over everything. Had we lived in a higher tax bracket, the well-to-do residents might have carved a protected area out of the forests bordering our home. But the woods around our blue-collar neighborhood would soon be clear cut, the footpaths turned to cul-de-sacs, and the box turtles smashed flat along with a bit of the wild and natural in your five-year-old dad. It was there, amid the bulldozer smoke and roar, that I saw, for the first time, something alien.

And the oddest thing was this: it looked like me.

What I saw that day started before I was born. *I'd rather have a light than a tree.* It was deep in the cultural aquifers long before this particular machine "enhanced" our particular forest.

On that morning—the morning where I lost the innocence of a child who thought he was equal to all other creatures—it maneuvered levers in an air-cooled glass chamber. It dwelled apart from the breathing humus. It wore protective goggles over eyes exactly mine. For the very first time, I spied Separation.

Daddy,

Reading these first letters, I've been seeing Separation in all kinds of places now. Like in this kind of weird thing that started at my high school. We've been joking around, calling each other cimento *or* atardecer. *It started when a couple of kids were saying, "Let's go over to the Piray River and catch the sunset," and another group was like, "No, let's check out the mall."*

So now it's all: "She's 'cement' because she only likes malls," or "He's totally 'sunset' because he'd rather go barefoot in the river."

It's just a funny thing we say to each other. And maybe it's no big deal. But I can imagine a scary future world where all teenagers have forgotten there's a sunset. But we haven't.

The story of Giggi taking you to search for box turtles reminds me of you teaching me to catch frogs. One time it was twenty-one frogs I caught in our Samaipata pond with Lukka. Remember that night? We were out there for hours with headlamps and put them all in a bucket. Four different species! We showed them to you and Melissa and then let them go. I still remember the moonlight gleaming on the pond as they hopped back in.

When I start to feel down, I know those frogs and the moon are still in me. Atardecer.

Love, Amaya

II

Source

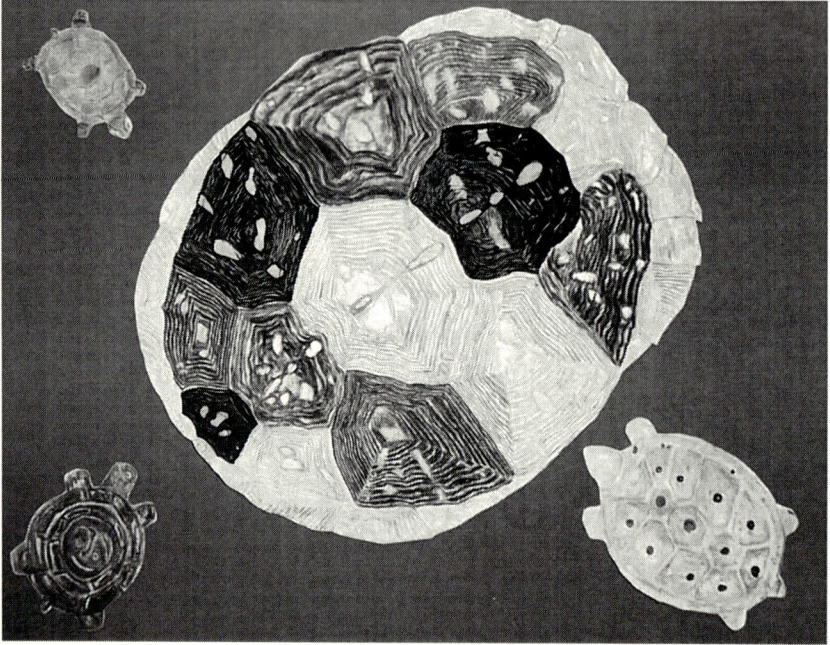

Four

Initiation: *Hay Luz*

Dear *Hija,*

When you were three, I lived in a rental house here in Samaipata, and you'd visit me for stretches. That was before I'd met Melissa, before we purchased land in Samaipata and built our family home. One morning, the dawn light streamed onto the bed where we'd fallen asleep together the previous night, and you were the first to notice it. You nudged me, saying: *"Hay luz." There's light.*

I muttered something about "ten more minutes," and kissed your small cheek. But the truth is this: I was *already* awake, busy being yanked around by my thoughts. I don't remember what particular cocktail of anxiety had moved from my dreams into my first waking minutes, but I was somewhere else: a darker place in my ego, and I hadn't noticed the light all around me.

You opened my eyes. I noticed sunlight streaming through the window. It illuminated the bougainvillea terrace and a radiant Piray River tributary shimmering beyond. The light gathered intensely around the garden you and I had been cultivating together: squash, green onions, and flowers. The day before, a Quechua neighbor had joined us there. He told you about how his ancestors farmed, suggested some changes to what we were doing, and then reached into his pocket and passed some seeds into your tiny, cupped hands.

There in the bed next to me, you were quiet for a moment, but then insisted: "*Ya no es noche,* Daddy. *Es día.*" *Night's over, Daddy. It's daytime now.* So I followed you. Outside into the luminous everyplace where spirit meets clay, where we grabbed tools and pressed seeds into the soft world.

You and I have already talked a bit about initiation, or rather the lack of it, in our culture and in your life, about how you're not being initiated into the life force the way your mom's Amazonian Tacana indigenous, and my Celtic ancestors,were. Your Bolivian *abuela*'s Tacana rites took fifteen-year-olds into the lush Beni rainforests for survival rituals, and emerging adults received specific scars and piercings to bring them into biocentric tribes.

Your Pop's Celtic ancestors sailed to southern Ireland in the twelfth century, hailing from syncretistic Christian-pagan communities in Gaul where the French version of our name, Powers, used to be *Pauvres*, or "poor." Our name didn't refer to material poverty, but rather to being "poor in spirit," a state of humility where a person acknowledges that true goodness comes from the divine, not from our egoic selves. Go back a thousand years in our Pauvres family-history book, and it seems young women your age in our part of Gaul went into sacred groves with their elders. There they were consecrated with a new name in their covens or other groupings. The actress in you would love how our ancestors played out—in the form of drama and ordeal—community tenets of encounters with the gods and inner transformation. Water was also seen as sacred. Initiates garlanded natural springs with flowers out of respect for water's life-giving properties.

Ancestral initiations at the critical threshold of adulthood—where you are now—once connected humans to the chattering spider monkeys, somersaulting oak leaves, and effervescing springs. The Bolivian Quechua word for initiation captures what fifteen-year-old humans have long undergone. The Quechua word is a composite of *yachachiy* ("commencement") and *wañu* ("death"). Coming-of-age, in Quechua, is *yachachiywañu*: *Die and begin.*

What dies? Childhood ends and a new phase begins. You take a fresh new role among your tribe and within a community. Could the illusion that we are separate from all else also die? Perhaps today that is the true coming of age, no matter how many years a person has graced this earth.

Modern culture has mislaid initiation rites, but we can renew them. We can reimagine the *quinceañera* within a deeper natural and cultural history. Initiation into the song of the world is neither esoteric nor exclusive. Connecting with nature is the default for every creature . . . humans, too. Even the people today who may seem the most disconnected have a deep-rooted life force in their genetic makeup and in their family tree. All of our ancestors, *everywhere* on Earth, arose from cultures that were animist. Their societies wove humans into the animate life force instead of imagining they could thrive outside of it.

I remember a couple of years back when Melissa and the mother of one of your Samaipata friends gathered you and your friend—along with a seventy-five-year-old woman friend from the community—around a bonfire on our land. You each were thirteen at the time and had recently had your first *lunas*, the start of your menstrual cycles. Tucked away in my study, where I could smell the smoke rising from the fire and catch glimpses of its glow, I pictured the women doing what they have long done: creating an open space in nature to share among different generations.

You later told me that the experience resonated with you somewhat and that, while you knew it was a caring gesture, it was *okay, but not great*. I pictured the strained, sidelong glances you and your *amiga* must have exchanged, the awkwardness around the fire you and your friend shared at times, but also clamped up. Perhaps the moment felt "tacked on" to a modern culture almost barren of such rites.

That particular attempt did not resound with you, but our world nevertheless requires experiments in ways to initiate ourselves into the life force. For your *quinceañera* I'd love to return to you the inner wisdom that you gifted me with that special morning when you were three and showed me the light. As you struggle now through an inevitably rocky teen phase in a world that is also increasingly darkened by Separation, I trust the *Hay luz* consciousness is still in you. As you turn fifteen, let your birthday gift be something that nobody needs to give you. You have it already as a body beside a river awash in moonlight and firelight, within a family beside a fire, eardrums tickled by tumbling water.

One of my students, whom I'll call Kaitlin, recently told me about a string of suicides in her California suburb. One of the American study-abroad undergraduates I teach and supervise in Bolivia, she'd walk up to our land in Samaipata to talk about her research. One afternoon, when we were done discussing sample sizes, twenty-year-old Kaitlin got quiet, her face strained.

We sat cross-legged on a hillock on our five acres, and I could hear the familiar murmur of the nameless creek, a Piray tributary, that flows through our eucalyptus stand on its journey to the Amazon and the Atlantic Ocean. Kaitlin finally confided that she was on antidepressants but often felt low anyway. "Disjointed" is how she put it. This is common among my students, including those who, like Kaitlin, attend *excellent colleges* and hail from *good families*. A half-dozen kids from the suburban high school she'd graduated from, she told me, took their own lives at different points that year by stepping in front of trains at a particular railroad-highway crossing.

The wind churned through leaves overhead, the creek warbled by us, and I pictured trains crunching human skeletons. "I knew a few of those girls," Kaitlin finally continued. "They seemed normal. Even happy. But one of them confided in me once: 'What's the point of life? *You live and you die and that's it.*'" How shocked I felt to hear those same words.

Kaitlin then added: "The parents at our school set up a twenty-four-hour watch over that railroad juncture. Sharing timetables on a phone app, they . . ." Her face flushed. "The parents protected the tracks."

Like the women who gathered with you around the fire, I'm struggling to do more than protect the tracks. I, too, may fumble as I grope to communicate these thoughts and feelings, and about things that are quite dark. My longing for you—and for Kaitlyn and so many others—is that you might better see and navigate today's confounding world. I long for nothing less than your survival.

Amaya, a lot of my students are on the same tipping point where Kaitlin was. And it's not that they were neglected by their parents or completely deprived of nature. Separation is far more subtle and insidious. A lot of my urban or suburban students, for example, had their own version of your own "Samaipata" as kids. Maybe it was in suburban woods or at a summer camp that connected them with fun in nature.

But sometimes our best efforts as parents isn't enough. I find that a lot of students get *an inkling* of this deeper love of the life force—of biophilia—but the collective imagined order so thoroughly conditions them that they feel in limbo. They're not initiated into an essential search, into an identity beneath the one society gives them by default—as workers and consumers in the capitalist system. I'm talking instead about another kind of identity. You might call it an *identity of natural existence*, where young people come of age as part of a territory and with a sense of vocation tied to their deepest inner voice.

I've experienced that sense of limbo too. Your dad was raised on the knife edge between the enchantment of box turtles and the horror of Separation crushing them; between a family's biophilia and a suburb's alienation; between a Firebird's supposed glory and an essential freedom I sensed but could not embody in tribe.

The very good news is that recovering rites of passage in our culture is more workable than it may seem. Initiation, the Quechuas' *to die and begin*, is always right here, right now. And not long ago, the Covid pandemic presented individuals and communities with questions and priorities born of destabilization—literal and figurative death, as well as new beginnings. The late Japanese Zen master Shunryu Suzuki once put it starkly: "When you do something, you should burn yourself completely, leaving no trace of yourself, like a good bonfire." He doesn't mean destroying the body, of course, but rather burning what's Separated within it so that life may preside. Here's an exercise I sometimes use to attune into this:

~~~~~~

Find a comfortable seated position, close your eyes, and ask yourself, *Who am I?*

Like a bird-watcher, wait to see what emerges. Perhaps nothing for a while. Then you might think, *A high-school student,* or something else. Ask again.

Whatever comes up, just notice it and repeat inwardly, *Who am I?* Each time simply ask the question, listen to the answer without judgment, let the answer go, and then ask again. Try this for ten minutes. Then you might do it each day for a week.

~~~~~~

In my own experience, each answer tends to deepen. I feel myself begin to expand, like a hot-air balloon slowly inflating. Some of my students who have done the exercise have said, in various ways, that it helps them relax into a broader reality and retouch a sense of inner peace.

A few years ago while on a trip to Washington State, I hiked to a spot beyond the imagined order. The professor in me would love to take you there on a field excursion, along with Kaitlin and my disjointed younger self. We'd journey to a place deep in the Olympic peninsula's Hoh rainforest reserve.

When I finally arrived there, scraped and exhausted, a grown-over sign led me up a path through the redwoods well above the river to a place marked by some good folks as the only place in the continental US where no machine makes a sound at any point during the year: one square inch of silence.

You won't find such a place in an American city or suburb. Nor within earshot of any road, nor even in a national park with airplanes flying overhead because such locales register disqualifying decibel levels. That left this single spot in the far northwest corner of the country where a single weekly flight plied the sky: San Francisco-Fairbanks. And do you know that those good folks convinced the airline carrier to reroute that flight so that one square inch of silence might remain?

It may not seem like much, one square inch within a nation, but perhaps even the least niche is enough: a place with no car alarms, ringtones, not even a purring refrigerator. Perhaps that one square inch of silence is inside each of us, in the continents of our bodies, a square inch where no marketing drill has perforated. A square inch where we don't need the Sierra Club nor Outward Bound because there's no plunder, where there are no chipped beings, no liquids smarter than blood.

This square inch is inside of you, and it is wild. For most of us it's a forgotten place, somewhere on the edges of our inner territories. Take the risk of journeying toward it, *hija*, even if most of the signs are grown over. You'll drop baggage along the way, perhaps everything you thought yours, and you'll get cut and bleed, but when you arrive, you'll begin to be free.

The most important thing of all is that when you discover your one square inch, it will be trillions. There is no scarcity of silence, just as there is no scarcity of the life force. We are—life is—profuse. Even in the noisiest, most Separated situations, you can plumb the ancient ocean that is your body. Infinity goes in both directions, and it's unlikely any nasoscope will ever find your floor. Why wait for a big culture out there to create rites of passage for you? While it's true that a wiser society than ours might someday possess the key to our innate joy, that joy isn't locked up. *Our eyes are the world's biggest thing.* And there is so much *luz* to take in.

Here in Samaipata, an otter swims across our shimmering creek. I'm rapt as I watch its sleek, long body move. Through my window in the small adobe *casita* where I write, I see—all around the otter—*carnival* and eucalyptus leaves falling into the river, dimpling the bright flow. The otter scampers onto the far bank and vanishes into the woods, and the sunlight I feel on my arms also illuminates some leaves I've cut out of undyed, handmade paper.

The cutouts resemble the real ones touching down into the Bolivian river outside. I wonder: might those leaves be the trees' way of speaking? Perhaps each tree writes on water through ripples, an infinite succession of *O's* ringing out. Some of these words drift downriver, but most settle onto the forest floor to dissolve back into humus. Traveling leaves and sedentary ones, they all melt into the life force.

On my desk sits a watercolor set and several brushes, and now I wet the paints. After some moments of absorbed awareness, I brush something on one of the paper leaves.

Dear Hija

Light spills through the trees as the early sun brightens the hills beyond. I gaze at the inscribed leaf as it fills with sunbeams. Then I choose another paper leaf and, in blue, write, *Quinceañera.*

A leaf falls outside, writes on water, streams toward you. *Yachachiywañu, my love. Die and begin.*

Five

But Can You Want
What You Want?

Dear Amaya,

Remember your classmate's dad at the school Father's Day picnic last year? When he asked you what you wanted to study after high school, you replied, "Theater!" with your typically mature stage presence, adding that you wanted to be an actress.

When he replied, he didn't know that being an actress has long been your dream. How extraordinary your poise when, at eleven, you played the lead in the musical *Annie* in front of hundreds in Santa Cruz's main theater on the central square. That self-assurance continued as you embodied characters as diverse as Oedipus in a one-act Argentine adaptation of *Oedipus Rex* and the Witch from *Into the Woods* over the following years. In your free time, you've taught yourself a rippin' ukulele. In fact, you've always been creative. At ten, while visiting us in Samaipata and attending a neighbor's birthday party, complete with live music, you seized a horse jawbone retooled as a rattle and jumped up with the adult musicians, keeping perfect rhythm with them, song after song. A grandmother there tapped me on the shoulder and whispered in my ear: "*She's* an artist."

When your schoolmate's dad responded, it was with a good-natured smile: "It's great you have a gift, but don't forget that there are other ways to share your gift than as a professional actress. You may end up poor." He looked at me and shrugged, then looked back at you. "Don't forget you could also find a *solid* profession and then act as a hobby."

To that dad, for example, our family's philosophy and daily culture might be hard to understand. It's like your story of how you and your friends joke around calling each other "*cimento*" or "*atardecer*." How to understand "sunset" choices when your perspective is "cement"? And there's a big vice-versa in that question, too!

There's a potent phrase in Bolivia: *Caminar preguntando,* or Ask your questions. Did the Covid pandemic get you considering wisdom questions afresh? How might you "ask" any new meaning-of-life ponderings and queries this week, letting them to inhabit your mind, yes, but also your senses, your bodily movements, your everyday tasks.
What would it feel like, right row, to not know?

The theater-skeptical dad at your school might appear, on the surface, to be well adjusted to Separation, but perhaps he *would* get what we're exploring here. Samaipata, for example, is full of folks who once led lives similar to his. The next time I ran into that dad, a few weeks later, he confided that he's far from status-quo blissful. Hailing from a working-class back-ground, he now sells Amway products for a living. This company, and dozens like it, are new to Bolivia. He joined the US company's pyramid scheme in Bolivia early and made quick and significant money that has vaulted them into Santa Cruz's top socioeconomic tier and a new gated community.

However, his family's financial foundation is wobbling today as Amway falters globally, particularly in Bolivia. With his family's everyday economy rooted in that company, he confided in me that he detests the quasi-border wall separating his condo from the outside. I think he feels trapped in a system where even the "winners" within Bolivia's gated communities are cordoned off from nature: their outdoor space paved with cul-de-sacs, their prefab dwellings filled with electric screens. The stress of all of this is exactly what is causing him and his wife to question things.

Several years back, when I'd returned from Bolivia and was living for a time in New York City, I got on the A train toward Central Park one afternoon and overheard somebody say, "Dude, that game's fresh!"

I looked up to see a twenty-something hipster in baggy pants, fashionably tousled hair, and what looked to be the latest Nikes.

"Yeah, it's awesome," replied another guy, equally cool. "Buckshot, right?"

"Yeah, Buckshot. It's just like ten dollars or something in the app store."

"I'm on that!"

I noticed our fellow riders tuning in to this animated exchange. When people experience someone enthusiastic about something, we become curious, and we mirror their excitement. Brain scientists call this phenomenon "neural mirroring." All the more so, it would seem, when one is eavesdropping and serendipitously hears about the Next Awesome Thing.

But something seemed off about the exchange.

The train pulled up at the 14th Street station. I watched the two hipsters get up, say "later" to one another, then exit. I rose to look out the door. The hipsters did not exit to the street, but, rather, reentered the next subway car through separate doors!

Going into private-eye mode, I left the train car and followed them. Unnoticed, I sat down several seats away from where the pair had reseated themselves.

Stand clear of the closing doors. The train rumbled north. My heart clicked; I was spying. For thirty seconds, the guys were quiet, one of them thumbing his phone.

"Dude, that game's fresh!"

"Yeah, it's awesome."

A *Groundhog Day* feeling paralyzed me. Reality hit the repeat button.

"Buckshot, right?"

Exactly as before, folks tuned in, neural-mirroring the excitement. I computed: two minutes between stops, thirty play-acted conversations an hour, an average of a dozen people overhearing it. That was three-hundred-something trend-setting New Yorkers, every hour, hearing from an impartial source about a hot new product.

I rose, displeased. Holding the hand railing as the train jolted forward, I walked in their direction, my indignity mixing with anxiety.

"I'm on that!" one of them said.

"You sound surprised," I interrupted. "Almost as if you didn't have the *same conversation* a couple minutes ago."

"Whatever," one said.

"Are you guys *marketing*?" I said, my heart pounding.

I was talking too loudly. "You just did the same spiel in the car in front of us. I followed you here."

Everyone's eyes were on us now. "You a stalker?" the other dude said.

I was boiling, but they weren't. Why should they have been? I'd just announced to everyone, in an unsteady voice, that I'd been following *them*. The train slowed, stopping at West 23rd. "Plenty of *locos* in this town," one said. Then they said "later" to each other and exited.

I slumped back down into a seat. *Stand clear of the closing doors.* The train rolled on, everyone averting eye contact with me. Still worked up, I tried to explain to the passenger next to me about "stealth marketing." I had recently read about it, but had never experienced it: a commercialization of the space of overhearing, where companies pay actors to name-drop their brand in parks and on sidewalks. I fumbled to explain what had *really* just happened.

But he, a fifty-something man who seemed to have heard it all, just nodded, indulging my fantasy for a minute before going back to his *Daily News*.

In a haze, I exited the subway in front of the shops at Columbus Circle and strode beneath the CNN billboard clock toward Central Park. I wondered: do we even need science fiction to paint us a world of Separation where corporations dominate? At that moment it felt to me that we'd already arrived at the point where people, unaware, tick along to the mantra of: *You live—you* consume—*and then you die, and that's it.*

Yachachiywañu. Die and begin. Let your own words bubble forth as you brave the animate waters of a wild human heart.

Stealth marketing illustrates how Separation *inhabits* both our social context and our inner selves. Psychologists point out that the root of many people's mental health problems today is Nature Deficit Disorder. While they are correct that "NDD" results from a deficit of mountains and wild foods, of flower-sprinkled meadows and waterfalls—in other words, *a shortage of a human being's natural habitat*—the diagnosis fails to probe more hidden aquifers. Separation resides so deeply within us, that it's not as simple as connecting more to nature in our daily lives and in our coming-of-age rituals. What's overlooked is that we ourselves are part of the "nature" that is each year more efficiently mined.

The process of Separation has led to a startling new development: our inner selves have become the world's most valuable extractive resource.

Last year, advertising investments surpassed mining revenues for the very first time. At $800 billion, advertising and marketing outlay *topped the combined net worth of the world's top fifty multinational mining firms.* Capitalism has long plundered gold, tin, silver, and now lithium for cell phones, tablets, and "renewable" energy. But now we humans ourselves—the solitude of our inner thoughts and feelings—get mined for profit.

Light glinted off the nickel-sized metallic device held up by a forty-something executive from Hewlett-Packard keen to outclass Google's chip in the brain. He enthused: "We'll put one of these on every dolphin in the Atlantic. Then we'll be able to track them as part of a single global digital brain we're making."

Living in New York at the time, I had taken the afternoon

to attend the Carnegie Council technology panel discussion in midtown Manhattan where he spoke.

Appreciative nods filled the room, but numerous people squirmed in their seats. A few even frowned. I think the HP executive felt the disquiet, because he added: "By knowing exactly where the dolphins *are*, we'll be better able to *save* them." His caveat quelled some of the uneasiness.

When the panel ended, I boarded the E train downtown to NYU to teach my Sustainable Development seminar and asked myself: *How does this become the new normal?* That panel took place some fifteen years ago.

Back then, I developed the habit of sharing, at some point in each of my classes, a paraphrased quote from Emile Durkheim, the founder of sociology: *You can have what you want. But can you want what you want?* On the day of that panel, I wrote Durkheim's phrase on the whiteboard, then looked out into a seminar of students from five countries, all of them in their twenties, perhaps similar to a seminar you might take in a few years. It was our third class. I noticed a few of the students shift uncomfortably in their seats, a squirming similar to what I'd witnessed at the technology panel.

Finally, Rick, a twenty-four-year-old Midwesterner, said: "I don't get it. How could I not *want* what I want?"

Tempted to speak, I waited. Silence filled our small classroom, tucked into a remote third-story corner of the 1913 Woolworth Building in the Financial District. Nicole, an activist from Oakland, raised her hand. "Well, Durkheim was a sociologist. So, if our desires are *socially* controlled, then maybe it's about whether or not we have *individual* freedom."

I nodded. "Can anyone give an example of that?"

"iPhones?" said another student, James, from Guam. "Like how there's a newer one always coming out." He pulled an iPhone out of his pocket. "I felt self-conscious about having the old one, so I did go out and buy the new one. And then, okay, I had what *I* wanted. It felt cool to have it."

He paused. "But Apple's marketing—and peer pressure from others who have been conditioned by their marketing—have in part *created* my desires. So who knows what I might have *really* wanted in the first place. I mean . . . if my desires hadn't been conditioned by that company."

I immediately gave James an A for the entire course. I'm joking, but he and Nicole were among the few students who really got Durkheim's insight. Similar to those fish in the parable, this is the "What the hell is water?" conundrum surfacing again. It's not something you solve with your mind, but, rather, a meta-level problem solved by gaining enough distance *to see your mind*.

A common response from my students to the Durkheim quote is: *Sure, I admit I swallow plenty of ads and PR, but that stuff doesn't affect me much. Why? Because I'm jaded enough to see through it all.* The students consider themselves media literate and, therefore, able to want what *they* want, not simply what the broader society wants them to want.

But it makes me wonder: would companies invest $800 billion in marketing each year if that investment did not get us *to want what they'd like us to want*? A parallel question: would the world's top fifty mining companies spend nearly that same amount if they did not unearth something salable? The behaviors multinationals extract from us through marketing are not as visible as commodities like iron ore and diamonds, but trillions of dollars of collective spending are. Aren't our *wants* extracted, guided, and monetized?

Growing up on Long Island, long before the constant social media onslaught and stealth advertising, I wasn't immune to this kind of conditioning. Pleasure, vanity, and excitement coursed through my teenage veins every time I saw an ad for a T-top Pontiac Firebird. On television and billboards, it beckoned: *We build excitement, aggressive performance, sensational looks . . . What price glory?*

The price of glory turned out to be most of my earnings from summer and afterschool jobs and a fractured focus that took away from nature- and study-time. But back then I felt something akin to love for that car. I thrilled to the sound of its engine, the smell of its interior, the dark sheen of its paint. Even the firebird symbol spoke to something in me that yearned for freedom.

Marketing promises us more than just thrills and freedom. It also pledges to save us. Marketers call *fear* "a robust motivator" since fear tactics create uncomfortable sensations in us which are then relieved by a given product or service. One approach is the fear of missing out, or FOMO, identified by phrases like "one day only" or "only a few left." Such calls to action emphasize that time is critical, so consumers need to act fast. Lawyer ads use fear to urge would-be clients to call their attorney's office first to avoid being "robbed" of potential millions by insurance companies. On an even more dire note, medical advertisements wield fear to stoke our anxiety that not using a certain drug or service will result in severe health problems or even death.

Years back I taught preteens in New Mexico to deconstruct advertising. New Mexico was the only state in the US that mandated media literacy for all public-school students. But my job didn't last long. Industry lobbying revoked the mandate: apparently, media literacy was too "subversive," perhaps because it helps us to learn to want what we most deeply want, sans corporate conditioning. However, while that window was open, I developed an educational experiment that proved effective. I'd record that year's Super Bowl commercials, then play them back in class so that my twelve-year-old students could analyze each one according to the six primal triggers: fear, pleasure, sadness, love, vanity, and excitement.

I'll never forget the first ad I showed them. Amusingly, it was for Pampers. Not ten seconds into that first commercial, three students simultaneously called out: "Love!"

I'd scheduled the "mothers and newborns" industry for the following week. Nevertheless, their alert minds grasped the fact that ads featuring *love* target our mammalian desire to take care of those closest to us. They'd already learned that love—like fear—is a deep emotion that drives vigorous consumerism. Mining our core desire to provide for our clan, marketers then channel it into a solution only their products can deliver. Such ads feature families, pets, or happy couples. Market sectors like jewelry, pets, and—yes—the baby industry typically tap love.

Those kids continued to floor me. Ad after Super Bowl ad, they identified which of the six triggers was working mini-fantasies on them. I imagine those students, now adults, are less vulnerable to corporate ops in their interiors.

But being able to want what you want gets more vexing still. Even if media literacy were to be taught to all twelve-year-olds, it doesn't negate the fact that each of us has already ingested an average of two hundred thousand commercial messages by the time we're that age. On the bright side, entire nations like Sweden, Norway, and Greece have enacted bans on all advertising aimed at kids under twelve. Such policies are based on research showing that young kids' brains are unfair targets, too tender to distinguish fact from fiction.

To practice your own media literacy skills, watch any ad and ask yourself: What's the promise and what's the lie? (Are they the same?) What do you have to believe about yourself–particularly about your "deficiencies"–in order to "benefit" from the product?

Is there another, possibly free way to meet that need? Or was it a need at all?

Employers looking at resumes don't tend to hire personal power and depth of perception. Instead, they look for the ability to handle tasks that aim toward higher productivity. This is the case in much of the corporate world, but even in nonprofits, Melissa and I have observed how many NGOs and UN agencies with which we've worked become ensnared in donor- and government-driven objectives, and therefore peg human resources into specific slots in order to implement those objectives.

Even seemingly positive concepts like "creativity" nest within a marketplace groupthink. We parents and professors, meanwhile, do little more than help you and your friends adapt to a job market driven by global standardizing forces, instead of allowing you to know your natural self . . . and then allow that perception to bubble forth into your work.

We can't *want what we want*—and not just because of the algorithms pushing our deepest buttons or because we never had a media literacy course. It's more fundamental. Marketing changes us *indirectly*, by affecting everyone else in our real and virtual social networks. In each social interaction we tend to condition each other into the Separated collective order.

Thinking back again to the interaction at the Father's Day picnic, you hinted to me later that your friend's dad's words began to pinhole-puncture your deeper dream. I noticed that you began replying differently to the recurring "What are you going to study in college?" question. "Theater," you'd offer and then add: ". . . *and communications*." This amended answer might sound more solid, and if it's what you wish for at your core, then it's your path. But what would it be like if, instead of pursuing a presumed solidity, you aimed toward *fluidity*? After all, you're no cyborg programmed into societally construed goals; you're an organic body that is more than half water. So why not *ripple*?

> Imagine for a moment that instead of orienting
> yourself within the Story of Separation you
> instead drop a pebble into the human. Then, when
> somebody suggests you trim back intuitions that
> feel true, you hear such propositions in the way you
> now hear other forms of human-taming, like social
> media ads and billboard messages: as a sort of
> background noise. Like Gandhi, you begin to know
> your naturally fluid center–the "still, small voice
> within"–to be your only tyrant.

If your inner voice ripples out *theater*, pursue that, living frugally. For a time. At a given point you may perhaps hear another answer and flow on to the adventures and challenges offered by that different path as it perhaps merges with your theater vision. Why not simply observe—from a still place within yourself—all the roles you've played and all the voices that have reflected back versions of who you might become? A grandmother's awe whispered, *Amaya's an artist.* More importantly, there is a stillness within you—the life force—that will speak in its own voice.

I love a parable that speaks to this: it's about Mahuda, an independent young woman who lived in a small village in the near East. Mahuda made her living by selling vegetables in a busy market. She was comfortable enough and liked her work. But one day the angel Khabir—you could think of Khabir as one's inner voice—appeared to Mahuda and told her to jump in the river.

Without thinking about it, Mahuda leaped into the water.

She was carried downstream until somebody on shore threw her a rope and pulled her out. That woman offered

Mahuda a job in her shell-fishing business and a small room where she could live. Mahuda appreciated the woman's kindness and took the job, working at it, rather happily, for three years. Then "Khabir" appeared to her once more and told her to move on.

Mahuda obeyed immediately and walked from village to village until in one place a man offered her a job in his fabric shop. This was new to Mahuda, but she took the job, learned the trade, and worked there relatively happily until the angel appeared again and sent her on. Mahuda worked at odd jobs for years in this manner, always moving along when that still voice instructed. When Mahuda was an old woman, she had gained the reputation of a holy person. People began coming to her with their illnesses and worries, begging her for a cure and counsel. One day a visitor to his village asked her, "Mahuda, how did you get to where you are now?"

Mahuda thought for a moment and replied: "It's difficult to say."

It is difficult to say because the top skill on Mahuda's resume was her openness to the directives coming from an angel whose name means *the all-aware*. Mahuda had the precious ability to react flexibly, attuned as she was to the life force, personified here as an angel.

Hija, the parable, to me, suggests something that feels true: We have an inner sense of destiny, direction, and vocation if only we listen deeply. Again, as your grandmother's wise friend put it, you're an "old soul," and you hear messages deep beneath the noise of today's Separated imagined order. The word *vocation*, after all, comes from the Latin *vox*, or voice. What would it feel like for your work, my beloved Amaya, to flow from your silent inner voice?

When you were ten, and Clea was two, I purchased a bag of wheat kernels for the two of you from a shoeshine man on the Santa Cruz plaza. We'd come from Samaipata to visit you that weekend. You fed the white, gray, azure blue pigeons as they landed on your hands, devouring the seeds.

I took a photo that day, and it's one I prize. It's always on my desk. Today it's next to the newest paper leaves I've been watercoloring for you. *Huy Luz,* reads one. Another: *The World's Biggest Thing*.

Now I pick up the photo. In it, four pigeons, startled by church bells, explode from your right hand and seeds spray onto cobble. Clea looks up at you, astonished, as your auburn hair flies back in the gust of pigeon wing. Your eyelids seem to fly back, too, your eyes madly joyful, everything scattered. Behind you Santa Cruz's cathedral spires rise. The basilica's broken clock is doglegged to a perpetual five sharp, but your childhood ticks on. Now it must end.

I put down the photo, and an idea surfaces from within me. I watercolor a single word onto a final leaf: *Ripple.*

Then I take the painted leaves down to our nameless creek, which flows into the Piray, and toward where you are today in Santa Cruz. Other leaves already travel the stream's currents, glinting light as they accept nature's course. One by one I drop my leaves in, too, along with this *quinceañera* wish for you: May *your own* words bubble forth as you brave the animate waters of a wild human heart.

Six

Future Zarahs

My beloved *hija*,

I promise to tell you about the knife I owned in New York City, and what I did with it in the streets on a rainy night. It's connected with the meanings of your name.

But that's further downriver. There are other stories I'd need to tell you first, including ones I've never shared with you, partly because they echo a sense of shame inside of me.

Before you were born, I was a relief worker in the coastal West African nations of Liberia and Sierra Leone. While serving in the latter country, I was forced to make what may have been an impossible choice, the kind of choice that results in someone's death either way. It's a story that shows how difficult—but ultimately how important—it is to discover one's own way to remain aware of what you once called "the world's biggest thing" and thereby see through Separation. It's a tale about discovering how to balance the heart with the natural mind.

You've told me you want to go to college in the US. When you accompanied me a couple of years ago on a college lecture tour I was giving in the Midwest, on one campus—your favorite—you said: "I actually have to *wait three more years* to come here? I'm ready *now*, Daddy!" Though you're independent enough to go to college at fifteen, there's something vital you've probably yet to learn, and it's central to who you are as a human. It's not discussed on the college tour, and it's something that may take you more years and lived experiences to internalize. For starters, it involves a base humility and gratitude that keeps you connected to your own humanity and to the larger world around you—a world that will offer you not only joy and inspiration but also, inevitably, sadness and suffering.

So many elements of our society, from friends to smart professors, will try to pull you away from your base humanity and condition you into Separation through distraction or intellectual argument. Take this one incident among many similar ones, from a seminar I took as a graduate student before I left for West Africa:

On the first day of International Finance, we introduced ourselves one by one in the seminar circle, and one of my classmates, from Thailand, went out on a limb and told us why he wished to work in humanitarian aid. He got emotional when he shared this well-known parable to illustrate his desire: *Two friends arrive at a beach covered to the horizon with marooned starfish. "Their numbers are so vast," one friend remarks. "Nothing we do could make a difference." The other reaches down, picks up a single starfish, and heaves it into the sea, saying, "It makes a difference to this one."*

The professor, an economist who'd worked at the top of the US Department of the Treasury, took this in, stony faced. Then she said, directing her comment to the group: "Forget those doomed starfish. Don't waste time tossing back a few. Instead, *prevent* future starfish from getting marooned in the first place. Cut the starfish death rate by 10 percent, and you'll have rescued a million instead of a handful."

I chose aid work because, a bit like that Thai student, I wanted to ease suffering—others'…and also my own. As a kid growing up in a Long Island suburb in the 1980s, I wondered how I could live happily in a world where I had so much and others so little. Or, as I'd later come to phrase the same question: how could I lessen the dull ache of estrangement I felt between myself and the rest of creation? I hadn't yet become the angry, muddled young man who took a knife out into New York City's streets. I wasn't aware of how my subconscious aquifers were being mined by a civilizational Separation, nor that I held an innate power to liberate my inner space. I think I mostly wanted to wiggle free of a narrow ego and stretch toward what I felt to be a fuller self.

But years of pleasing professors like that economist for grades, and then as a young aid practitioner, had turned my "humanitarian" yearning into something a little outside the human. After Georgetown, I was sent abroad with a large nonprofit to lower rates of starvation, infant mortality, and HIV transmission; and I'd come to focus on numbers, not individuals' pain. Human beings had become statistics to me—and perhaps not without reason. If I'd truly seen every starving child as an actual starving child, it would have overwhelmed me into inaction. Relief organizations aren't the Peace Corps. The Peace Corps doesn't send volunteers to the countries where I used to work, the so-called "Fourth World" places where the globalization beast barely pauses to wipe its lips. These are places mired in war, or just recovering, with no sign of a government or the most basic elements of safety that so many enjoy in other parts of the world—places like Sierra Leone in 2004.

That's where I met Zarah. I'd been hired as program manager by a US aid group, which helicoptered me into Sierra Leone with a mandate to help rebuild the country's demolished healthcare system and reduce maternal mortality. A ten-year civil war had just ended, and women in Sierra Leone continued to die in childbirth at a rate *two hundred times higher* than that of American women. In fact, the country had the world's highest maternal-mortality rate, worse than Iraq's and Afghanistan's: two dead mothers for every hundred births. My job was to put together a team of thirty people to build clinics and train birth attendants so that more mothers would live to raise their children.

My team was put in charge of Sierra Leone's poorest region, the hilly rainforest state of Koinadugu. It had no functioning public sector or public utilities, only a few paved roads, and spiking HIV, TB, and malaria rates. Imagine trying to build from scratch a healthcare system for a Vermont-sized area with only four jeeps and half a million dollars at your disposal.

We had been working ourselves to the point of exhaustion for two months when my mud-covered jeep passed through the village of Fabalah, and a man suddenly stepped in front of us, waving his arms. Our driver narrowly avoided hitting him.

"The girl dying!" the man said in English.

My colleague Meg and I jumped out and followed him between mud huts with zinc or thatched roofs. Meg was a twenty-six-year-old nurse from Illinois, and her idealism was more intact than mine.

As I entered a hut behind the man, the swollen silhouette of a girl took shape. This was Zarah. Meg brushed by me and fell to one knee at the girl's bedside. Zarah's big belly looked ready to burst from her pregnancy, and bright red bumps covered her swollen legs. Sucking at the air, she strained to answer Meg's questions. Meg took Zarah's pulse. It was all she could do; the village had no medicine or equipment.

"This girl is going to die," Meg said.

"How long does she have?" I asked.

"Hard to say. She's basically allergic to being pregnant. She needs to get to a hospital with a blood bank. She needs a cesarean."

I rushed back to the jeep and got on the radio to our office in Kabala, Koinadugu's capital, but the situation there wasn't much better: the state's sole ambulance was presently in the nation's capital, Freetown, along with Koinadugu's only two doctors.

Palm trees swayed in the hot breeze. I felt lightheaded. My joints ached, and I hoped I wasn't getting malaria again, not out here, beyond drugs and IV drips. The irony of this thought, in light of Zarah's plight, would strike me later.

Back inside, Meg was whispering into Zarah's ear and stroking her forehead. I led Meg into the adjoining room.

"Should we turn back, take her to a hospital?" I asked.

"Your call."

She was right: it was my call. Though still young, I was the senior official. As I'd learned on similar occasions in the field—and as you'll inevitably experience as you come more fully into adulthood—nobody was going to make this decision for me. The dilemma would provide an ethics professor with enough material for a thirty-page journal article, but I had just minutes to make a decision. I looked through the doorway at Zarah. A hundred villagers who had gathered around the hut were staring in the windows. Though contorted in agony, Zarah's face was beautiful. Only a few years older than you are now. Nineteen.

I wanted to turn our vehicle around and take Zarah to the nearest hospital, six hours away in a city called Bo. But the hardened professional in me was programmed to think: *Forget about the doomed starfish at your feet. Cut the starfish death rate, and you'll save so many more.* I couldn't run an ambulance service here. I needed to be realistic. If I turned the jeep back, I'd be abandoning our work in another village: training birth attendants, distributing malaria-preventing mosquito nets, and overseeing the construction of a clinic—activities that could save dozens, even hundreds, of future women from Zarah's fate.

The three other jeeps that fell under my program were too far afield to assist. One had been stuck for a week on the far side of a flood-stage river, where our staff members were now subsisting on what they could hunt or forage. Only one other vehicle passed through Fabalah each week: a truck from Guinea spilling over with goods and people—no room for Zarah. I could either go on with my work and leave her to die or save her only to agonize later over the dozens of unknown women I'd likely condemned to death.

I knelt beside Zarah's bed and touched her forehead: hot as fire. I felt the heat build in my own face, and—despite years of experience with this kind of situation—tears rose to the surface. I tried to envision the faces of all the women we'd save by continuing with our mission, but the only one I could see was Zarah's. I whispered to her that I was sorry. It was impossible to turn back. There was nothing we could do.

That evening I spent a sweaty, sleepless night in Mongotown, three hours from Zarah's village. I imagined Zarah's body swelling. I imagined her, conscious and suffering, aware of her own imminent death and of her child's. I felt like a failure—or, worse, a killer.

I cursed the way international aid is hardwired for failure, like putting a drop of iodine on a full-body burn. The US was at that time spending roughly a *hundred thousand times* as much on the current war in Iraq as it was on development in Sierra Leone. We aid workers are fig leaves for a wicked foreign policy rooted in Separation: round up a few idealists, give them a few bucks and some jeeps, and maybe somebody will think the world's governments care. On top of that, the irony stung deep as I reflected on how one world order oversaw the colonizing of Africa by white men, then engineered Sierra Leone's losing hand in an increasingly globalized consumerist world, only to then send another white man—me—back to "save" the women who were taking the brunt of this centuries-old sacking. I felt sick to my stomach.

That long night in Mongotown, the forest around the village was silent. The infamous Colonel Cut Hands had terrorized this area during Operation Feed Yourself. Rebels kept the population in line by cutting off kids' hands. Rumor of their barbarity caused villages to empty out even before the advancing rebel forces arrived. That's how they secured their objective: control of the lucrative diamond fields.

There's a kind of mythology around African wars that turns them all into ethnic battles, but Sierra Leone's was much more about the global economy—more about *global Separation*—than about local tribes. The country, including the healthcare system that could have saved Zarah, had collapsed into chaos in large part because Westerners want to adorn their ring fingers with diamonds. We effectively finance warlords like Colonel Cut Hands by buying so-called "conflict diamonds." With a little political will, we could boycott or even actively embargo diamonds from Sierra Leone, Angola, and other war-torn countries, but we don't. "Embargo diamonds? Are you *nuts*? Diamonds are a girl's best friend."

Tell that to Zarah.

As the night wore on, I felt I was playing a fool's game, sent into impossible situations with comically inadequate tools.

The next morning at dawn, pinks and reds illuminated my mud-caked jeep, and the sight of it reminded me of the mosquito nets and birthing kits inside, and of the clinic to be built. I worked straight through until noon, unable to stop thinking of Zarah.

The sun had reached a fierce, scorching peak when I spotted Meg approaching across a clearing.

"We've got another one," she said breathlessly, indicating a group of women in colorful dresses huddled around a body stretched out on a *kente* cloth.

"How bad?" I asked.

"She's thirty-two weeks and bleeding. Went through three pads. If she doesn't get to a hospital right away, she'll lose the baby."

Twenty-four hours earlier I would have done the cost-benefit analysis and left her behind. But something had changed during that sleepless night.

I walked across the clearing and looked into the girl's pained eyes. I bent down and listened to her breath rise and fall. A cloud moved across the sun, the heat eased, and a breeze blew across the treetops. The women gathered around me, and I could feel their collective energy. No theory I'd learned seemed applicable. "We'll take her," I said.

As we bumped along the road toward the state capital, I felt doubts grow inside me. I'd leapt into unknown waters. It was impossible to run both an ambulance service and our long-term programs, but the very impossibility of it gave me renewed energy. As poet and philosopher Paul Valéry wrote, "A difficulty is a light; an insurmountable difficulty is a sun." I'd work on Sunday, my day off, to make up for the villages I'd miss today. The boundaries of the possible suddenly looked more flexible. I told the driver to take a detour back to Zarah's village.

Zarah was still alive when we reached Fabalah, though she was moaning more now and had bloated further. As I rode on through the jungle terrain, with a pregnant girl on each side of me, the only challenge was getting these women to a hospital before either of them—or their babies—died. The two women hadn't been washed in days, and their smell was overpowering. We opened our windows and let the humidity pour in.

Not an hour later, one of our tires burst with a pop. In the time it took to change it, Zarah's moaning stopped. I tried to nudge her awake. No use, though she was still breathing.

We were quickly back on the road again. I'd radioed ahead to the state capital for a jeep, and one was waiting to transport the pregnant girls to the Bo hospital and to take Meg and some other health officers to a distant project site. Though the new girl was no longer losing blood, Zarah was barely conscious. Using old foam mattresses, we improvised a cramped bed in the back of the new jeep. I put one arm under Zarah's leg and another under her neck and lifted her. She felt surprisingly light, as if bloated with air.

The smell of decay filled my nostrils. *Could I be exposing myself to what she has?* I thought. *Who cares*, I answered, as I placed Zarah gently onto the mattress.

I didn't know it then, but I was coming closer to something I'd later think of as *the life force*. I was becoming more human. Swimming away from Separation.

As their jeep raced on toward the hospital, I headed back into the interior, where another clinic was ready for inauguration. When I pulled up to the whitewashed building, a brilliant orange sun was already low in the west, and stars and planets were peeking through the darkening sky. I stepped out into a dancing crowd and the sound of drums and voices singing joyfully. They pulled me into the celebration, and we danced right into the marvelous new clinic. When the music had stopped, the chief gave thanks for the simple cinder-block structure, which had a well for safe water, a latrine to eliminate feces from underfoot, and a solar-powered refrigerator for medications.

But I couldn't fully join the celebration. These folks didn't see beyond their village to the ten thousand other villages in Sierra Leone without clinics. The rates were back at the forefront of my mind. The *rates*.

I got up early the next morning and headed toward another village. On the way I raised Meg on the radio and asked what had happened with Zarah. The response was garbled. I made out only a faint "Zarah," and then static.

Hours later Meg's voice drifted into the jeep, sounding wavy, as if underwater: "When we dropped her off at the hospital Zarah was—" Silence, then static.

"Negative copy," I said. "Please repeat that."

After an interminable pause, I heard Meg's voice: "Zarah was still breathing."

The jeep hit a deep pothole. My insides jarred. *Zarah was still breathing.*

Dear Dad,

Zarah has been with me today. The story got me thinking about my own education, how privileged I am to get to attend a great high school. But then what's next? It's college, and then the j-o-b . . . (How Separated am I anyway?!?)

When you started as an aid worker, you seemed to struggle with how to reach out to future Zarahs, and that's what they're already drilling into me in econ and math and geography. But if I keep getting trained to be in my brain, how do I keep my heart open?

For me, my body's instinct is powerful, and it's important to do what I feel most driven toward. Decisions are difficult when I lose my core.

On my bedroom wall, I wrote the below to remind myself.

The Present Moment

III

River

Seven

Re-tribe

One clear morning when you were nine, after ten minutes of helping Melissa and me weed our Samaipata corn patch, you stopped working and leaned resolutely on your hoe. It was the beginning of a vacation, and you'd just arrived from the city. You announced in Spanglish: "*Esto me recuerda de un* movie." *This reminds me of a movie.*

"Which one?" I asked.

You drove your hoe half-heartedly through a *quiñe* weed, then said, "Those movies . . . where the people, in the old days, worked in the field *todo el día*, from sunrise until sundown, never stopping to rest."

Melissa absorbed what you were saying and began to giggle. Then I started laughing and so did you. Finally little Clea troweled sand into the air and screeched, making us all laugh even harder.

It wasn't always easy for you to adjust to this—your dad's—family culture, which differs from your urban days in Santa Cruz. And it *is* kind of funny: After all, why the heck *were* we swinging hand tools in an Andean field?

That was a number of years ago, and by now you've spent abundant time in Samaipata and know your family and our community. It may even feel ordinary now—simply how your dad and stepmom live and how you live when you are with us—so I'd like to share with you a little of our tribe's hidden anatomy.

For years, Melissa and I have explored how to "re-tribe," so to speak, beyond Separation. We do this today within our Bolivian migration spot's unique social and natural ecosystem.

We rehabilitated our five-acre territory which, when we purchased the land years ago, was almost dead. For the two previous decades it had alternated between intensive cattle pasturing and chemical monocrops. Through "permaculture" techniques—that is, agriculture and landscape design in harmony with nature's forces—our family has accompanied the land's transformation from a thorny, barren landscape of hard-clay soil, to a lush arbor full of wildlife and edibles.

To do this, we planted hundreds of fruit and forest trees, hauled in manure and compost, channeled water through the acres using acequias and swales, and built a bio-constructed home which harvests rainwater and recycles sewage into the roots of banana trees. We also created—out of the hole where we dug the adobe bricks for our home—the pond you love . . . where you caught the twenty-one frogs with Lukka!

That wasn't your first frog search. You initiated several of your friends into this activity, and your first time was when you were nine. You and your friend Wara stayed up until midnight catching frogs in that pond's moonlit water. "We caught *twelve!*" you announced, when you and Wara came inside with dancing eyes, mucky to your waist. It thrilled us to see you repeat the midnight-frog-search fun during different sleepovers. Clea watched you then, and now imitates you as she catches frogs and nets catfish in the Piray River, releasing them into what has now become a fishpond stocked with six hundred tambaqui fish for part of our pescatarian family protein and also to sell in town.

When you were small, you adored not just frogs but also . . . *bugs.*

Many nights we'd take jars and a net out onto the terrace and trap lightning bugs and beetles, morphos and giant ladybugs, all attracted to the porch light. We'd observe this flamboyant range of forms, sizes, and colors, part of the niche ecology of our home at the elbow of the Andes, where they nudge into the Amazon. Thanks to you, I came to appreciate our local biodiversity more sensorially.

I've never talked with you about this, but in parenting you and Clea over the years, Melissa and I have more accurately been *childing,* as we've asked questions like: how do we foster family life which is more part of nature's web? How can we allow a simpler kind of parenting to emerge which allows our children to bring us back into the here and now?

You and Clea have long loved the creek that flows through our land. These days Clea often hears its gurgle before I do, at times childing me out of my very adult to-do lists. *Splash. Gush. Gurgle.* Onomatopoeia waterfalls through her vocal folds. As David Abram puts it: "Our own languages are continually nourished by other voices—by the roar of waterfalls and the thrumming of crickets . . . Language is a sensuous, bodily activity born of carnal reciprocity and participation."

One day Clea reached the water so ecstatically that she stripped down for "nake-nake" time. "*Wawa!*" she cried out, mixing two languages, her conjunction of "*agua*" and "water" conveying the stream's voice. *Wa-wa-wa* splashed into a pool, leaped into a two-year-old's inner ear, ricocheted off her pink tongue. Her bare feet entered the flow. Following her, I tore off my shoes, too, to together *wawawa*.

Melissa and I have tried to create a spur-of-every-moment childing culture in our family, and it includes practices like family counselor Naomi Aldort's WAIT (Why Am I Talking?). I use it sometimes:

> When I'm about to either put a label on a mystery or try to make a challenging situation right, I WAIT. In other words I ask myself: "Why Am I Talking?"
>
> I sink into the sky, a breeze . . . and also into my inner weather. Something fascinating usually happens: The moment aligns. Life doesn't need Mind.
>
> While it is not a panacea, WAITing is a good tool that anyone can use, even in moments where you feel most pressed upon or inadequate. The simple act of refraining from speaking has a "Let go and let God" effect of releasing a person, temporarily, from ego.
>
> Can you think of a situation where you might adapt this practice to your life?

WAITing helps me to be biocentric—two sisters, and a daddy, too. In the best moments, this helps me appreciate how attuned you or Clea can be to your senses as you notice a hawk overhead or stop to pick red dahlias.

Do you remember that bright-sky morning in our Samaipata orchard when we planted your persimmon tree?

You and Clea each got to choose your own tree sapling. Clea squealed "peach!" and you announced you'd love persimmon—and we did a tree-planting ceremony where you two sisters bonded with your saplings. Today, each time you come home to Samaipata, from your other home with your mom and grandma, you measure yourself against your tree. It is finally taller than you. I love the recent photo where your head of unruly hair is crested by the persimmon's leaves.

It's hard to forget that look in your eyes on the day of your tree planting. A few friends had gathered for the ritual, including your sister's godmother, Melissa's close friend Casimira Rodriguez, an indigenous Quechua union leader and former domestic worker. Casimira led a traditional *ch'alla*, or blessing, for our new house and orchard, and then, beside your newly placed tree, I recited a bit of John O'Donohue: "Alive to the thrill of the wild, meet the dawn on a mountain . . . Become subtle enough to hear a tree breathe."

The look in your eyes was open, intelligent, and probing as you sank into the meaning of this ritual, your eyes seeming to ask: what is my connection to this land, this *ch'alla*, this "breathing" persimmon sapling I've just planted?

That particular ceremony, one of many rituals woven into our family's life, links us to homeplace through specific fruit trees.

Our family—you, Clea, Melissa, and me—comprises more than a nuclear family. We swim within a spirited Transition town.

Samaipata belongs to a lightly associated Transition Network, launched in England in 2008, in which size varies a lot. Our town has five-thousand inhabitants, but Transition streets encompass a single city block. Today, sixteen-hundred Transition initiatives thrive in fifty countries. They are grassroots community initiatives that seek a changeover to a post-carbon lifestyle where local self-sufficiency helps reduce the effects of climate change and global economic instability. Instead of waiting for governments to act on our behalf, Transition communities get homegrown in renewed approaches to energy, waste and recycling, food production, and transportation, showing by example that life beyond Separation can be liberating and fun.

Back in 2015, Melissa and I, together with some friends—a mix of folks born in Samaipata, along with migrants from elsewhere in Bolivia and abroad—watched the documentary *Transition 2.0*. We discovered that all we needed to do to join the Transition movement was get a core group to declare an intention to form a local initiative and then take related practical steps. So we did just that, inviting trainers from Mexico and Spain to facilitate two energetic days called "Transition Launch."

In a room packed with our Quechua mayor, town councilors, businesspeople, and students, we spent the first day envisioning our community deepening itself as an "ecological municipality." The second day dealt with Inner Transition, as we meditated and did interpersonal exercises like author Joanna Macy's "work that reconnects."

In the months after the workshop, many action-initiatives like eco-governance, group purchasing, and green energy took root. How exciting it was to feel freshly linked with the friends I'd bump into on the plaza or in our town's seven-day-a-week "farmers market"—which in rural Bolivia is still called simply, *el mercado*, or "the market," since there *is* no supermarket within a two-hour drive. There we'd share ideas for the organic agriculture and recycling policies we'd dreamed up together and were now helping to birth. And how cool it was to see your Samaipata friends—like Soami, Wara, Ginger, and Lukka, who are also turning fifteen—and their parents, in very differing ways, as part of our larger "family," one that, in a sense, has been co-raising you in every visit you have with us. Our families, though quite different, have increasingly exchanged DIY products from our gardens and orchards and shared know-how in household green energy and greywater reuse.

Re-tribing and Transition are bumpy. Melissa and I have sometimes found it hard to escape our Western conditioning into efficiency and individualism. Local Samaipata friends have often come to our aid. An example of this, which I adapt from my book about Samaipata, *Dispatches from the Sweet Life*, is something that happened during Carnival seven years ago, when we were gifted ten new tree saplings.

Carnival in rural Bolivia in many ways celebrates interconnection. It involves *festival*—a key element of community—with a nod to the natural, a celebration of the harvest. In Samaipata, parade floats with *comparsa* queens and ambulant brass bands stroll down Calle Bolívar in a multigenerational extravaganza, as children, parents, and grandparents dance together in matching smocks and hats. Some of the floats are themed around the harvest or *Pachamama* (the indigenous Bolivian word for Mother Earth). As the February corn matures on hundreds of small plots around the town, so too do carnival groups flourish with their maize-themed ensembles. Six years back, a friend, Pedro, passed me a bottle of the corn-based, home-brewed alcohol called *chicha*, which I swigged and handed back into his dancing group as they passed by.

His float was decked out in blossoming carnival-tree branches, and on a pedestal, the queen wore a crown of the buttery yellow flowers. Later Pedro, in the festive spirit, gave us the gift of ten treelets in little black bags—five palms and five carnivals.

The following morning, a warm one with the sound of brass bands playing below in town, I macheted through an area near our creek and dug holes. For weeks I'd been studying our go-to handbook, *Permaculture: A Designers' Manual*. The book's pages were frayed, and I'd double-underlined this sentence: "Every element must have multiple functions, and every major function must be served by multiple elements." The sentence felt liberating. *Nature will work for us!* Do you remember my excitement to get out on the land and plant trees? That's what I felt the day I, while laboring, envisioned the single "element" of the gifted tree saplings as one day serving three functions: a windbreak, a pleasant view, and a source of palm nuts. I'd been sweating for two hours to attain the *Manual's* element-to-function ideal when a friend, a thirty-something Bolivian horse-tamer with little formal education, named Kusi, stopped by.

She watched me. I waved but kept grunting away in combat with the underbrush. When I glanced up again, I noticed a slight smirk creeping up one side of my friend's mouth.

I put down the machete, picked up a shovel, and began digging another palm tree hole. Looking up, I saw Kusi's smirk had swelled, and I felt a little annoyed. Finally, I blurted out: "What is it, Kusi?"

Unhurried, she ambled down the slope toward me. Saying nothing, she began to pick up felled baby trees. A tiny *tipa* tree. A *soto* sapling. I was appalled to see I'd hacked native trees from where they were naturally growing in order to put in the foreign ones Pedro gave us. Kusi still hadn't said anything. She continued to assemble a little mass grave of the horticultural newborns I'd slaughtered.

I felt silly. Steeped in permaculture *theory*, I'd been clearing out the undergrowth without bothering to look at what was in it. Kusi picked up the machete and gracefully edited away grasses, spiky *quiñe*, and scrub tula trees, leaving behind two tender carnival trees, one of them winking with a single yellow flower.

"Don't sweat," Kusi said to me. "*Uncover.*" For the next hour that Carnival morning, Kusi and I uncovered what was already there: a future forest of diverse native trees, many, like the tipas, with medicinal functions. We brought to light more carnivals with the most gorgeous flowers and scents. We uncovered spaces without any naturally occurring saplings, too, and that's where we placed Pedro's palms.

LA DESTRUCCIÓN AMBIENTAL NO ES DESARROLLO

EL HUMO TIENE RESPONSABLES

Eight

A Local Future?

Although our family grows much of our own food—like in those movies you mentioned!—and have built a carbon-light house using a blend of indigenous and contemporary bioconstruction techniques, we're still embedded in global capitalism. Even as Melissa and I aspire to "uncover" nature's abundance through tapping "radical homemaking" income streams like selling our crops in the market and bartering the jam, kimchi, and honey we produce with neighbors, we still have to make much of our living through online work.

Indeed, Separation comes to our doorstep all the time. Take a recent April afternoon in Samaipata: It was a week after the pueblo had eased its way out of the annual fun and the chicha-hangovers of carnival and gotten back to work. I found myself rounding Calle Campero, my thoughts on a new local currency we were developing to encourage local purchasing—the "Samay" you, and over a hundred of us in town, now use—when I noticed a change: the yellow carnival tree I'd usually see from that point on the street was blotted out by something colossal and red.

Puzzled, I continued walking toward the plaza. Our town sundial was also blocked by what, from that angle down the narrow, cobbled street, looked like a bloodshot massif. Curious, I quickened my pace, noticing that the intrusion had also rubbed out any view of the church and family-owned shops on the plaza. Finally reaching the plaza, I saw a hundred fellow community members gathered under a two-story, inflated red bottle emblazoned with "COCA-COLA."

To the pulse of reggaetón, some of our neighbors pushed toward the free soda bottles handed out by attractive Coke employees, teenagers from Santa Cruz. A local nine-year-old you know, Pablo, approached me with caffeine-wired eyes and exclaimed: "My sixth!" I was amazed to see him swill the rest of a bottle, then open his schoolbag to reveal a stash of Cokes. Pablo ran back up to seize another. At the same time, other people scoffed at the effort, saying *"No, gracias"* to the free samples. They didn't need a media-literacy course to spy the subconscious trigger in such addictive flash marketing: pleasure. That, along with a bit of FOMO: the employees in their branded shirts shouted, "Only a few more left!" Twenty minutes later, they deflated their pillar and motored off to the next town.

This scene captures how thousands of us in Samaipata, collectively, are in many ways exactly where the rest of the world is now: embedded in individualism, weakening traditional and indigenous values, overwork, consumerism, status, and fossil fuel dependence. You're an astute teenager who readily spots hypocrisy of all kinds! Not only is global consumerism right here in Samaipata, but it's inside me and Melissa . . . and inside indigenous Samaipatans too. We're not creating a utopia, some kind of pure ideal. Nevertheless, I know you've tasted a bit of what it feels like to experiment in living out an ideal, flaws and all.

That's why, even as Coke and other multinationals try to "add life" to Samaipata—through the promise of better taste, sound, and color than a natural existence provides—Transition gives us at least *some* antibodies to Separation. Localizers are at work, and at play, here, building a community that embraces spiritual awareness, a gift economy, and reduced energy consumption. This process is irresistibly nonlinear and enjoyable, even if it's far from perfect.

Dear Dad,

Years ago I sat in the Samaipata plaza strumming my new ukulele. I struggled with the chords but had fun playing the tune. I thought I was alone when a man whose face I had never seen before approached me. It was clear he was a traveler passing through my town like hundreds that came before him. He was maybe twenty-five, and he had a charango *(a small, ten-stringed Bolivian instrument). He played along to the song I was trying so hard to learn.*

He challenged me to improvise new music with him. I was startled but I did my best and we played. And played! The moon rose, curious about the tunes, and her rays danced to the music. The rays twirled and pranced. They limboed between our strings. They held hands with the vibrations and resonated into the night.

The man asked me to join him again the following night, but I said no. "The weather forecast says it will rain tomorrow," I said, knowing that you probably wouldn't let me go out at night to meet some strange dude, lol.

He laughed and stood up. "My name is Amaru," he said, and told me the story of how he changed his name. Amaru means snake in Quechua. They said it was the animal that crossed worlds. Just like the snake, the musician Amaru kept crossing worlds. I never saw him again. The moon and I will never forget Amaru.

Samaipata is the exact center of South America. It's a crossroads. There's a constant flow of travelers going from one place to the next.

Amaru and other people I've met in town are artisans, selling homemade things, and that's partly what inspired me to do DIY. I remember how happy I felt selling my own jewelry in town, with Clea as my assistant!

A few summers ago, I was selling jewelry under the sundial, and I asked Soami's dad if he wanted to buy one of my bottle-tab earrings. He said, "No, I don't want one." Then he smiled and said, "I want five!"

I only had four pairs of earrings so I whipped pliers out of my artisan kit and made two more earrings while Clea showed him puppy Pandito's tricks. It felt amazing when he handed over a wad of bolivianos. And he was happy he had gifts for his wife and daughters. Clea and I sold more jewelry that day and the day after. I'm so psyched she started her own DYI business!

Dear Amaya,

Local economy is irresistible! What you felt on the plaza may be similar to the intimacy I feel selling our organic vegetables and herbs at our house with Melissa each Wednesday morning. A neighboring grandpa recently came by our land and loved the bagged blackberry, jasmine, banana, and honeysuckle plants I'd cultivated in our makeshift greenhouse, so he placed an order. The next day I wheelbarrowed the bounty over to him, and he handed me not a wad of *bolivianos*, as with the man buying your jewelry, but rather, payment via our Samai local currency app. I then used that same Samai to pay Leandro, the bike repairman, to come by and refurbish our family's fleet of four bikes.

A person doesn't have to read Eisenstein's *Sacred Economics*—although I hope you'll someday get into how negative interest rates, depreciating currencies, and the like can help seize economic power for local communities like ours—to *feel*, as you did, the sacredness of such transactions. Ones made in place, with people you know, in a dynamic cycle where value swirls locally and boosts nurturing community.

Granted, a Home Depot employee must feel a similar rush of well-being when she helps a customer find the right sheetrock and sees that customer go to the register and purchase it. We all want to feel useful in tribe, and that salesperson *is* being useful. But how much autonomy does she have over her own life? Where does the profit she helps to generate flow? What is the environmental impact of the collective order in which she's embedded? Would she be any *less* happy if she were selling, for instance, local adobes instead of chemical sheetrock and if those bricks were her own? Might this feeling of usefulness, of *belonging*, be deeper still?

~~~~~~

Fostering local economy begins with getting to know where you live more intimately, Begin by taking a walk around your neighborhood and just observe. Ask yourself, What do my neighbors or the land around us need? And: What can I offer?

For example, "little free libraries" and their pandemic variation, "little free pantries," foster small-scale local economy through an exchange among a small group of people responding to each other.

> Another example is participating in 55a CSA
> workshare to receive a discount, a CSA box, or a
> chance to cavort with newborn goats.

You've seen this quote hanging above the desk in my adobe *casita* workspace in Samaipata. It's from Canadian philosopher Marshall McCluhan: "Only puny secrets need protection of patents. Big discoveries are protected by public incredulity." One such *big discovery* is that humans can organize themselves into an infinite number of possible communities, instead of conforming to a single global monoculture. This is the pluriverse instead of the universe. It's the textured, diverse world currently resisting a UniPlanet under construction by multinationals and the political figureheads who serve them.

I conducted a study of Samaipata under this driving question: Could towns in the Global South—instead of being "poor" and in need of "Western-style development"—actually be models of sustainability and future-fit living? To probe this question, my research team applied the wonderfully ingenious *Gross National Happiness Index Survey*—based on the Gross National Happiness index of Bhutan—and the *Happy Planet Index* to our town, also calculating Samaipata's carbon footprint and per capita GDP. The result of the study is startling in its magnitude: Samaipata shows higher levels of happiness than countries that have per capita income levels seventeen times higher. Moreover, Samaipata's environmental impact is nearly seventeen times lighter than those same countries in the Global North.

I do such social-science research in part because our Separated world is so data driven. It's one thing to *say* to policy-makers that Samaipata offers powerful solutions for a planet facing grave and intersecting crises of unhappiness and environmental destruction, but it's another thing to *prove,* numerically, that incentives toward localization are crucial and that towns in the Global South contain insightful lessons for industrialized nations. The research shows that the *vivir bien*—or "living well"—economy and philosophy that have been the foundation of Quechua, Aymara, and lowland indigenous cultures in Bolivia for millennia are effective. It creates a positive societal norm of striving to meet only basic needs in terms of food, shelter, clothing, and work—to the point of living *well*—but then not striving toward a never-reached horizon of living *better*.

To reverse Durkheim, humans *can have* the communities we want . . . and also *want the ones we want* too. Samaipata is such a place. It's Don Rulas building eco-houses and German-transplant Ludwig blacksmithing furniture. It's Kusi freelancing in jaguar and Andean bear tracking—when she's not taming horses—or Doña Serafina opening a successful vegetable stall in the market. It's you bumping into Amaru and learning a sweet ukulele riff. It's those examples . . . times a thousand.

Latin American towns like Samaipata are, you might say, little anarchies. Large employers rarely come to them because the scale is too small to make money. Ninety-five percent of the ten thousand people in the larger municipality of Samaipata—our town plus the forty smaller villages and hamlets around it—are, therefore, entrepreneurs. "Separated" northern governments and mainstream economists have an unfortunate word for this: failure.

Oops, here I go lapsing into professor-speak again. But this is vital. The conventional story about today's Bolivia is that, in *failing* in the 1990s and 2000s to achieve the so-called "Washington Consensus" goals of liberalizing trade and opening up to foreign direct investment—that is, to induce big companies to come—Bolivia remains burdened with the supposed worst of all evils: a large "informal economy." But this failure is fruitful soil for rebel localization. Samaipata's informal economy is nothing less than freeholders like our friend Theresa selling her *empanadas* and Estuvio shaping his adobe bricks. It's the fifty women organic farmers with their farming cooperative sales point on Calle Bolívar and our friend Diego who runs the local radio station and emcees events.

This is not to say, of course, that large employers are bad. Jobs with good benefits are desirable and necessary today for workers like that Home Depot employee, particularly in today's corporatized Global North. Nor does affirming "informal" entrepreneurism in Samaipata and elsewhere in the Global South mean, implicitly, that companies should be deregulated, too. For example, extreme outsourcing—the social fabric-shredding way that companies swell bottom lines at the expense of worker pay and benefits—must, of course, be regulated.

But it's key to also see that the "multinational corporation" *is an imagined concept.* It can be reimagined as something more balanced with local economies. Today 90 percent of GDP runs though corporations, and a paltry 10 percent surges through Samaipata and other local economies the world over. What would the world be like were that ratio fifty-fifty? Positive substitutes to Separated economics exist now, like the small and beautiful economy, *hija,* in your own Samaipata. Such communities—which sustain people, Pachamama, *and* profit—should be cultivated more broadly in unique ways.

No, you don't have to plant a hillside corn patch or join Transition Samaipata to be part of the worldwide insurgency beyond business-as-usual Separation. In the United States and the rest of the Global North, millions of people today seek more Earth-connected, family-friendly, and leisure-rich lives on the land, in smaller towns, and within cities as part of a burgeoning *localization* phenomenon stretching far beyond the growing Transition movement.

This swell also includes tens of thousands of ecovillages, from Findhorn, Scotland, to Sieben Eichen, Germany; and from Muita Vida in Florianopolis, Brazil, to Dancing Rabbit Ecovillage in Missouri, USA. These thousands of unique but sustainability-aligned communities network together through the forty-year-old Global Ecovillage Network (GEN) that has matured to such a point that it's been invited into the United Nations system as a model of alternative localization economy and durable habitat. There are also tens of thousands more spiritual communities, *Cittaslows* ("slow cities"), and suburban and urban cohousing projects spanning the globe.

Hija, I know it's easy to feel a little hopeless. With the reelection of Trump, and with AI feeling so much more embedded in everything just in the last year or two, it can feel like localization is being shredded up in the capitalism woodchipper. But when I look at this, I sometimes come back to the Bolivian indigenous *el tercer incluido* ("the inclusive third") sensation where it's not simply a dualism of *either* corporate hegemony *or* thriving local economies. The third option *includes* both of these at the same time, and our gaze best focuses on the hope within the near-infinitely textured fabric of what's happening at all kinds of levels.

Consider—even in our seemingly dire McWorld—how community-supported agriculture (CSA) grew eight-fold in the last decade in the US. In fact, the recent boom in CSAs is indicative of the larger push toward local manufacturing and local supply chains. This trend accompanied a breakdown within industrial-scale meat-processing plants during the pandemic as CEO's fretted about essential and farm workers

staying well enough to show up for work. Sure, global consumerist forces are happy to slash corporate tax as they cut
subsidies for localization. Yet the CSA boom continues even
under Trump, as people learn about their food in their immediate region, its climate and seasons, and their neighbors and
local farmers. Isn't it possible that such seeds could be part of
what grows a sense of "biophilia" as we move toward the more
localized "Transition" manufacturing that experts have begun
to predict?

Okay, enough poli sci. In my heart, Amaya, I'm sharing this
intellectual analysis because, you could say, I've fallen in love
with the local and it's one of the ways to share that love. These
statistics and examples flow from yearning to share so much
of what we don't hear in the mainstream press. Or in movies.
Or almost anywhere else.

The other day Melissa handed me a faded snapshot of you
and me walking arm in arm, talking, down our local main
street: Samaipata's Calle Bolivar. You looked to be eleven, and
your face was half turned away from me, smiling as you divid-
ed your attention between what I was saying so earnestly and
the sight of the shop window we passed, *La Ranita* bakery.
You hadn't been home to Samaipata in months, and many
people shouted your name—including the man who would,
years later, buy those five pairs of earrings from you. Several
friends ran over to give you a welcome kiss. Though I don't
remember the exact stroll captured in Melissa's snapshot, I do
recall that, on our poker day, we went on to swap amusing
anagrams. Rearrange *Dormitory* and *it's a Dirty room. A deci-
mal point* > *I'm a dot in place.*

I share these recollections because of the subtle ways that
memories, too, compost into local human ecology. When an

economy belongs to a place, and to the humans collected there, economics is more than statistics and currencies, alternative or otherwise. Community itself is a living organism, self-contained and releasing the sense of happiness that any organism feels when healthy and integrated. Similar to how sight happens on its own when the obstacles to vision are reduced, well-being happens when Separated economic structures are lessened and real localism comes into focus.

An indigenous grandfather in our town captured this with much wisdom, one day, when I asked what the widespread Bolivian philosophical idea of *vivir bien,* or "living well," meant to him. That grandfather's deceptively simple response captured something of what you and Clea have long taught me about existing in the here and now. His answer also spoke to minimalism and the joy of re-tribing.

"*Living well,*" he replied, "is eating well, sleeping well, and loving well."

Nine

An American Transition Family

Dear Amaya,

Big news! I've arrived in Vermont.

   As I mentioned, I'm about to begin a writing fellowship at the Vermont Studio Center (VSC), to both withdraw into solitude and work in community with artists and writers on parallel journeys. It's hard to leave you, Melissa, and Clea behind. And for a whole month. But I'm doing this in large part because of my deep love for you—and also because of my deep concern for you and the world, as you're about to come of age at *quince*.

   Your wisdom and verve both delight and awe me, yet your milestone birthday heightens my sense of a perilous threshold as our species risks near-complete departure from the natural flow of life. I've realized I need to go *even deeper* into my one-square-inch of silence, and write from there. That's why I've journeyed here.

My sister Amy, her eyes and skin radiating the health of life on the land, picks me up at the airport. In her car we cross a Green Mountains pass toward her house, an hour's drive from my Vermont Studio Center residency; I start there in two days, after a visit with your *tía* Amy. We merge onto a valley road along the Winooski, a wide river coursing toward the Atlantic that gathers force through a hundred tributaries. One of those tributaries is Snipe Ireland Brook, which weaves through your *tía*'s ten-acre homestead in Richmond, Vermont.

She crosses Snipe Ireland on the way up her gravel driveway, and we pass a deer-fenced garden exploding in kale, pass the apple and peach trees, and park at a spot where your *tía*'s family's "dome home" comes into full view. Almost twenty years ago, your *tíos* bought a 1960s Buckminster Fuller-style, wood-paneled dome, and your *tío* Andrew, a skilled carpenter, hand-constructed an extension to what is now a five-bedroom house. There's no neighbor in sight, with the dome bordered by thousands of acres of protected forest along the Long Trail.

You've been here only once: We celebrated your second birthday here, with your mom, *tíos*, cousins, and your Giggi and Pop. But since you were too young to remember that, I'll share with you a bit about your Vermont family. They suggest how an American clan can quietly shift the collective order.

The front door opens, and I embrace your *tío*. He hugs me, all 6´2″ of his marathon-running, sinewy body. Then comes the warmth of your three cousins, each so distinct and confident. Leo, fifteen, is the quietest; he loves reading and hiking and backwoods survival. The middle child, Huck, is artistic, illustrating books and singing Broadway tunes. And, Roy, ten and a little stockier than the others, loves to tell jokes, enjoy treats, and care for his pet guinea pigs.

When our hugs time out, your cousins snap to their "contributions": they chop garden veggies, empty the compost bin, and set the table while my sister cooks. We then sit down on the porch to eat, but first little Roy rings a bell—a ritual you recognize since we have adopted it into our family—beginning the meal in silence with several deep breaths. During the meditation, Snipe Ireland Brook bubbles audibly below.

After eating, we amble the woods tracking deer and talk about a giant storm that's predicted to hit Vermont in four or five days. *tío* Andrew talks about the previous storm that hit Richmond, leaving some of their friends' and neighbors' Winooski-side homes severely flooded and now uninsurable. He half-jokes about things boiling to a point where—climate and economy increasingly derailed—local governments like Richmond can't afford to maintain present infrastructure, and fuel shortages leave but a few Vermonters able to afford private cars as "Central American-style chicken buses begin to ply a potholed I-89."

The next morning is Forest School. I walk down to the creek and spot twenty kids and several adults in clusters. One group builds a shanty out of stripped pine boughs, dovetailing in the corners. Another gathers wild plants by the brook. A third learns to skin squirrels caught in a trap handmade from sticks.

Forest School is a wilderness education program focused on play, nature, healing, and community. Your *tía* and *tío*, in community with other local families, helped dream up and implement it, and they donate the use of their land for it. But this is not just something that happens in a summer camp as an afterthought to "real" education. Forest School is one day a week throughout the whole school year—in sunshine, mud, and snow alike. Parents simply remove their kids from local elementary and middle schools, and drop them in the woods. Local school administrators—partly because they had little choice, the program having grown to nearly a hundred kids on multiple days—look the other way with respect to the truancies.

When I enter the clearing, Roy spots me. "*Tío* Billy!" he shouts, grabbing my hand and pulling me over to help gather hemlock boughs with which to make forts. Then Leo shows me the waterproof container he was busy forging out of pine bark.

I meet the lead instructor, John, who offers a forearm touch instead of an animal bloodstained hand, and tells me briefly about how the kids learn outdoor survival skills and appreciation of nature experientially through a place-based education philosophy. But he's quickly shuttled away by a nine-year-old asking whether a certain mushroom is edible. I watch John head toward the creek, dreadlocks to his waist and a skunk's coccyx laced into his dark beard. My sister, who is president of the environmental education evaluation company she founded, told me about the first time she saw John. "Our committee interviewed some earnest environmental educators for the Forest School post. Then John came to the interview. When he showed up barefoot, dreadlocked, with his bone-adorned beard, his kind eyes and gentle spirit, we knew he was the guy."

That afternoon we drive in their ordinary minivan into their apparently ordinary, American small town, Richmond (pop. 5,000), four miles from their homestead, for the boys' soccer practices. I watch *Tío* cheer on your cousins, and see the other soccer dads and moms in a huge multisoccer pitch, a gorgeous grass expanse beside the Winooski River, Richmond's round church steeple rising up across the bridge, and I can hear the water flowing during lulls in the cheering.

It's ordinary, and it isn't, the alternative school your *tíos* and some of these cheering parents support: Mansfield Cooperative School, which gets these kids out of Separated education and into creativity, all the while centered on an approach of not prepping classes toward tests, but inhabiting place. It's ordinary, and it isn't: the vibrant farmers market held on this field every week, the local and organic food in the Richmond Market on Main St., the fact that two-thirds of the area's food in the summer months is produced in local economies. It is ordinary—or perhaps it's extraordinary—that the state capital, Montpelier, a half-hour up the road, has experimented with Gross National Happiness as a state dashboard to eventually replace GDP. That means they measure the success of their local government on the well-being of its inhabitants rather than the amount of money that moves around. Like our Samaipata, Montpelier is a Transition town fostering organic farming, alternative energy, slow life, and local economy.

These trends are modernity, too, with the Latin *modernus* meaning "being current, of the present." Many Bolivians tend to equate US modernity with Miami-style capitalism, since television and social media in Bolivia mythologize Separation as cornucopia, even as developers build the first McMansions in new gated suburbs where some of your friends' families are starting to reside. That imagined order may seem powerful, but on the fertile fringes of empire bloom *"Rich-*monds" like your *tíos'—mundos ricos* of another other sort. What comes to light, on that soccer field, is the lived answer to the question I picture you someday asking, and the earnest one I often get from my university students: how can a handful of free humans possibly change what appears to be an unmovable corporate consumer society?

The peaceable revolutionaries that are your Vermont family skillfully undermine what passes in Separation for *I, we,* and *it.*

They begin with themselves, the "I." The pre-meal silent meditation is but one of a dozen deprogramming practices that have become part of this family's culture. The three boys not only spend the week in creative education but also have their summers expand with unscheduled time in the woods that is punctuated by wilderness-survival and meditation camps. Your *tíos* have meditation practices, too, and the whole family chops wood, carries water, plays musical instruments, and sings together—the brook's voice always present. With each thing they do, they harmonize with the song of the world.

Their inner acres thus gradually discovered, the family (the "we") is able to sculpt those portions of the material world under their control. They top their dome-home with solar panels—making it carbon negative as the panels produce all their own energy and also feed the community grid—and have for fifteen years used a composting toilet. Besides primarily edible landscaping and a tiny lawn mustaching the dome, they cede most of their acres to wilderness.

But what about their minivan and the highways on which they drive it daily? Since this portion of the material reflection of the imagined order is not under their control, it is none of their direct concern. There's a wise ancient Stoic dictum that's useful today:

"Ta' ephraim, ta ouk ephraim?" In other words: What is up to me, and what is not up to me? This means: try not negativity as you stay centered in your still, small voice.

A person in this state acquiesces to what can't be changed. In the end, Sapiens economic and social systems are but small subsets of Gaia. So humans are patient, shaping the material world where possible. But just as importantly, they don't create more Mind out of what can't be, at present, re-shaped by themselves.

For example, your *tíos* continue to have to drive a vehicle. But it's in a state of acceptance that they flow past strip malls and fast-food chains, waterfalling over the Separated ideas of pundits and politicians who buttress Separation. They're in it, to the extent necessary—but not of it.

Finally, to help shift the material order, your *tía* and her friends get together for clothing swaps where, without spending a nickel, each of them re-wardrobes by tossing clothes into the pile and selecting other garments. The family has also helped turn their Burlington-area food co-op into the country's second biggest community-owned and -run cooperative, generating millions of dollars annually through distributing hundreds of tons of healthy, delicious local food. They've also started the two new schools we've seen, but perhaps the loveliest collective practice they've birthed has to do with a hundred-year-old cider press. Every October they host a Cider Pressing Party at the dome, a hundred friends and neighbors taking turns to hand-crank the huge press and fill countless gallon containers for all present with the juice of mostly gleaned apples. A new communal order flows through this celebration of summer fruits and Earth's tilt toward winter. Or to use a metaphor from your theater training: it's a brand-new script, rich with improvisation.

Before your *tíos* drive me to the Vermont Studio Center, we reach you on a video call. As your image flickers up on the screen, I'm taken not just by how gorgeous you are, but more significantly by the confident young woman you are becoming, as you ask your cousin Leo what he's been up to.

"Not much," Leo says, all casual, until *tía* rejoins with a "Come on, Leo," and he describes his recent solo week in the woods. He walked out the back door with a pocketful of rice "just in case" and years of Forest School knowledge on starting fires without matches, harvesting edibles, and trapping small animals. Leo says he dined on burdock, cattails, and stinging nettle, and missed his family, "but it was great."

As your cousin shares this, I watch your expression change from amiable to baffled to bright eyed as you grasp the power of this sort of ancient-modern initiation.

When your *tía* says, "We'd love to have you come live with us here," you know what she means: the semester exchange we've talked about for years now, where you'd study at the cooperative school and on Fridays at Forest School.

I watch as your face lights up.

Ten

Then you leave,
and art begins

Dear *Hija,*

Walking through the still-unfamiliar town of Johnson this morning after visiting your *tíos',* I saw a little boy playing in front of his home, a tan duplex with paint peeling at the edges and around the windows. He looked about four, a softness to his face somewhere between toddlerhood and school age. Toys and a rusting bicycle were scattered around the patch of lawn between the sidewalk and his house, and the clear morning air smelled of sugar maple, birch, and pine. Singing "Baby Shark" under his breath, the boy ran and hopped from one toy vehicle to another as he crashed them. As I passed, I saw he'd shed his shoes and socks and was about to stick a foot in a puddle.

I smiled, reminded of two-year-old Clea and her ecstatic "Wawa!" moment in the stream and how good it had felt to tear off my shoes, too, and follow her into the water.

I lifted my hand to wave, but before I could greet the boy, a thin man with a shaved head threw open the front screen door. "*Don't* step in the water!" he hollered, and the boy yanked his foot away, silent now and cowering before his dad, who glared at me. I managed a midstride nod and a "hi" to the boy, who followed me with suddenly numb eyes.

Don't step in the water, a father says to his son, stealing away a moment of magic. But stolen by whom? Not by the dad alone. As with the theater-skeptical dad at your school picnic, I had a flash of wondering: *What field or forest did he run in once?* Another's suffering is an expression of universal human pain. If we are indeed one living whole, then isn't one human being with "a problem" really a wound in the common larger entity? And how am I to deal with the despair—for both the boy and his dad—that I felt after witnessing this moment, particularly after experiencing the wholesome, tender ways your cousins were being brought up in biophilia?

It's a predicament. Eight-*billion* individuals of our species inhabit Gaia now, and the power of just one of us to affect the whole is extremely limited. Yet many of us fall into the fraught "save the world" trap, which, however outwardly noble it may appear, tends to burn out the do-gooder who, through over-reach, ultimately accomplishes nothing. Hence, the archetypes of the stressed social worker, the jaded inner-city teacher, or the world-weary activist.

Instead of world-saving, there is a field of enlightened action beneath the rush to do. Both Einstein and Jung hinted at it when they observed that the world's problems can't be solved at the same level of consciousness at which they were created.

You know about enlightened action since you taught me directly about it not long ago. It was an instinct of yours that imparted so much to me. You certainly remember that time when you were almost thirteen when—during a visit to Samaipata—you were walking the perimeter of our land when the harsh slap of skin from over a neighbor's fence caught your ear. Then came a wail. We heard the cry from all the way over at the house. I ran outside as you came up crying. "He hit his kid!" you exclaimed.

You, Melissa, and I huddled to discuss this unexpected situation. Our first reaction was to call children's protection, but it was delicate. Though I'm naturalized as a Bolivian citizen, and you've lived in Bolivia all your life, it's a sensitive issue to call the authorities on your neighbors. Were we to do that, we might be accused of being outsiders arrogantly meddling. Also, the family was renting the adobe house and had just arrived a month before. We had little idea about their situation.

Maybe you recall what you did next: You were silent. We followed your lead, the three of us relaxing and listening to the warble of the creek. A flock of parrots flew noisily overhead. Something seemed to align. You suggested we allow a few hours to pass, then invite the kids—the family had four children—over to our orchard to play with Clea.

Over the coming weeks, we started doing that, and the kids loved the free, wild space. We also brought the parents a basket of vegetables from our garden and began chatting with them in order to get to know them. It turns out the dad was unemployed, and the mom was struggling with a housefull of young kids. After that, we never heard any evidence of abuse.

> What you did was an example of how Melissa and I have learned—including through your and Clea's insight—to approach problems in a manner both spiritual and practical: see, be, do.

Here's how we practice See, Be, Do: first, we see the problem. It could be anything, from resentment toward a family member, to a homeless woman by the curb, to a government plan to fund a bigger nuclear bomb instead of schools. I find it's easy to look away from such problems, because we're busy working, or feeling stifled or even apathetic because there is too much to do in general. But isn't each so-called problem there to make us stretch toward being more compassionate? Either we face the issue, and grow toward becoming more human, or it comes back again and again in one form or another.

Now the next step: let's say we've garnered the courage to see the problem; it's not yet time to act. Instead, we let things *be*. This is the hardest part: going to that solitary space of our one square inch of silence. Some people call this place God; others call it intuition, the "still small voice," grace, or simply "presence." The name doesn't matter. These are merely signposts for an experience we must come to understand directly. For example, imagine you'd never tasted honey. Somebody could describe "honey" for weeks and you still would have no real comprehension of it, but one taste would bring instant understanding. When we find a way—be it through meditation, music, a child's eyes, a shooting star, anything that brings us closer to the life force—to become present, we can then look at problems with fearless clarity. When the child next door wailed and you suggested we pause, you were lifting us into this space.

The final step—*do*—is then as natural as drawing breath. You hand the homeless woman a sandwich; form a peace study group in your community; invite the neighboring kids into the fresh space of an orchard to play. Or take one of a thousand other actions.

I've noticed over the decades that the people most able to blend inner peace with loving action have something in common. It doesn't seem to matter whether they are Buddhist, Hindu, Jewish, Catholic, or born-again agnostic. They tend to employ some version or another of *see, be, do*. Instead of allowing the negative forces of a Separated world to create more disconnection, they maintain beauty and control in their interior space through being fully present in the moment, and thereby release that clarity into the social world. Through conscious action, they cultivate what's human and put what's Separated in the background.

Traditional Bolivian culture is quite acquainted with seeing and being. For example, Quechua young people are required to live for a full year with their proposed marriage partner so they can *be* with the person and *see* the *chachawarmi* (combined male-female) dynamic before they *do* a whole lot of knot-tying. And I've noticed while working among Amazonian indigenous people that there is a ritualized neutral listening to particular community problems, followed by a period of silence. Only then are decisions made, and by consensus.

You and your friends, *las cumpas*, are connected culturally to those indigenous practices but are increasingly raised in a Western time-is-money world where *being* is a tough quality to cultivate. In the hustle of high school and beyond, a clutter of stuff and activity tends to eclipse the sweetness of solitude, the aliveness of the present moment. It's one thing to have the privilege to ponder enlightened action on the peaceful banks of the Gihon River or the nameless creek you love that flows through our Samaipata land; but, at fifteen, as you further enter the river rapids of climate chaos, the abuse of kids around you, and other inevitable trials, how in the world is it possible to stay centered in your still, small voice and *do* from there?

Yesterday evening, I attended a Vermont Studio Center "welcome talk" on art by Jon Gregg, the cofounder of VSC, and the parable he shared connected with this question.

When I entered the VSC Mill House dining room I saw some twenty other residents gathered. It was strange to be amid so many new people. I'd been secluding myself for the first days there, keeping to the woods housing my tiny studio over the Gihon and a spartan attic bedroom on the other side of the river. I'd remained on the fringe of this revolving tribe of resident visual artists (with a few writers tossed in) all of us gathered for a month here within VSC's collection of some two dozen buildings spread through Johnson. "The writer, that solitary animal," is how novelist Lawrence Durrell once put it; thus far at VSC I've been reconnecting with my one square inch of silence. Writing means abundant solitary time to do the work—even during the times when the writer would rather be with his family and in tribe.

Jon stood up suddenly. "When you start out as an artist," he said without preamble, "a hundred people are in there with you. They're crammed in, but suffocating you in the studio."

He pushed a pair of round glasses up his nose. The tall, curly-gray-haired man didn't seem particularly comfortable with public speaking. "Your parents are there, in your studio. And your brothers and sisters, your colleagues and friends."

He paused, and I looked around and recognized one other person at the far end of our semicircle, a reclusive painter, a Chinese woman named Feng Mian. Her dark blouse flecked with white paint, she appeared to wear some of the thousands of stars I'd seen her meticulously painting through her studio window.

"As you try to work in your studio," Jon finally continued, "your teachers and professors are in there, too. *Ogling* you." This unexpected description elicited muted laughter. Outside, large Shambhala prayer flags flapped in the breeze above the mill's falls. Jon and his wife, Louise von Weise, both artists now in their seventies, arrived in Vermont four decades ago to meditate with Buddhist master Chögyam Trungpa Rinpoche at the nearby Karmê Chöling Shambhala Meditation Center. With scant dollars in hand, the newly-weds risked taking out a loan to purchase a few dilapidated buildings in Johnson. At the time, they toyed with establishing either a meditation center with an arts component or an artist residency with a meditation component, eventually choosing the latter.

Jon ran a finger through his beard, as if thinking about what to say next. "The other artists who have inspired you, the 'great ones' . . . well, they've squeezed in too. It's suffocating. You can barely breathe. But, over time—it may take many years—as your craft and style grow, those people begin to leave your studio. One by one they walk out until there are only a few left."

He allowed the silence to build around us. Through the window I heard the warble of the Gihon beneath Mill House. Jon's low voice broke the reflective silence: "And then they walk out, too, and you are *alone* in the studio painting, or writing, or sculpting."

With this pause, it seemed that Jon had reached the end of the story. But he added one last piece, in a clear voice: "Then *you* leave, and art begins."

This potent sentence still rippling through me, I walked out into the chilly June evening and sought out the VSC meditation house. At first I couldn't find it, even in the clear moonlight, but then I saw prayer flags rising behind the wooden and metal shops and walked toward them. Half-hidden amid a cluster of tall bushes was a possibly twenty-by-twenty foot wooden house.

Leaving my sandals in the entryway, I stepped beyond a Japanese screen to the meditation space and felt a familiar sense of peace. The principal ornament was a weaving on the wall of a curious three-dot symbol, ⊙, as yet unknown to me. I wondered what the symbol meant as I lit a candle, sat cross-legged on a cushion, breathed with intention, and watched my thoughts.

Five minutes passed, then ten. My mind was crowded at first.

I counted my breaths—ten on the inhale, hold for
ten, ten on the exhale—meanwhile imagining each
thought as a soap bubble. I allowed each to float up,
then popped them one by one.

Doing this—simply seeing thoughts and "popping"
them—eventually made the spaces between the
appearance of these bubbles expand. Not judging
the thoughts, I focused on simply counting my
breaths.

The bubbles that floated up become less frequent.
After thirty minutes, I felt calm and clear.

Formal meditation is a sort of ceremony which brings us into
presence. Though ideally this state is brought into each of our
actions, a daily formal meditation ritual helps center us into
"water"—the life force—before or after we go about our day-
to-day activities.

I began meditating when I was a few years older than you
are now and have continued the practice since. I follow no
strict lineage and have had plenty of lapses. Meditation is not
a religion, but, rather, the most direct way I've found to connect to biophilia. While I'm meditating, the stress of too much
thinking gradually evaporates, and I begin to see *what is* instead of what my conditioned mind would like me to believe.

These days, when I'm at home in Samaipata, I do the following ritual every morning: stepping into our family meditation
room, I light a stick of incense, then ring a bell. From there, I

allow the thought bubbles to surface one at a time. In a neutral way, I name each of them "thinking." If my thought-emotion complex happens to be pulling me into negativity for a day or several days—our inner states, like the cycles of clouds, follow natural patterns beyond our mental control—I use another tool, visualization, to complement my meditation.

A recent visualization I made up fosters *maitri*, or loving-kindness: I picture being with you and Clea in our orchard, the two of you hugging me. Pandito bounds over into our laps. Some of my favorite local birds—a trogon, a golden-billed saltator—perch on your special persimmon tree, over our heads. A mantra-song that Clea sometimes sings echoes: "The birds love me, the trees love me, everything around me loves me, and *I love myself.*"

> I take the maitri sensation—which I feel as a life-rich green color emanating from my heart—into the intention: "Watch now as I start this day with happiness, with kindness."

It's hard to imagine this visualization going stale, but it will. Like water, our minds move and flow, covering different ground. As each ritual I've come up with over the years has become rote, I've changed it. I encourage you to experiment with meditation and visualization, perhaps even inventing a practice that works within your inner weather right now.

Hi Dad,

Sometimes I know the feeling you're describing. I feel it when talking to the wind or hearing the grass adjust to my body when I lay on it.

The feeling brings me back to when I was hiking in Colorado last summer. On Day Eight I touched the sky and it hugged me back. I froze in that moment like I was gliding over the mountain ridge into a new world. Usually I watched my feet while hiking, but this time was different. I looked up at the rows of mountains that sparkled under the sun.

The Continental Divide was covered by trees, colorful flowers, and the remains of old memories. I felt like a bird flying through the sky and we sang and screamed at the top of our lungs.

I wrote this poem that night in my tent: Hoy toqué el cielo. / Este me abrazó de vuelta. / Quien diría que las abejas viajan tan alto / Tan alto que desde lo lejos siento mi tierra? / Y su canto que me transmite el viento.

To remind myself of that moment, I wrote on my wall:

Don't think
about life
LIVE IT

Eleven

The Reef

Dear *Hija*,

After breakfast two days ago, I saw Tennessee artist Jasmin Bell tossing stones into the Gihon from Mill House Bridge. The thirty-something sculptor stopped to study me. I'd already gathered a bit about how the challenges of her life as a gay, African American woman in the Deep South had shaped her, yielding the profound artist she is today. Jasmin possessed some of the clearest eyes I'd ever seen, large brown ones reflecting the rippling Gihon. Unexpectedly, she invited me to visit her studio to see what she'd been making.

I crossed the bridge with her toward a building of visual art studios, and we climbed the stairs and entered her second-story workspace, a thousand-square-foot studio far larger than my scribbler's nook. What she'd done to it in the short time since we'd all arrived jarred me. Jasmin had transformed a bare, high-ceilinged studio into something . . . *entombed*. A full half of the large space was encased—ceiling and walls—in plaster and papier mâché, atop an understructure of thin bamboo and salvaged chicken wire. I traversed the studio and touched the pallid shell into which the room was morphing. The air felt drier on my skin and smelled of chalk. More than a sculpture, the space itself was *becoming* something else.

Jasmin pulled up some jazz on her phone, climbed a scaffolding, and got to work. I stood in the corner, between her studio's closet-sized bathroom and the window overlooking Johnson's Main Street, and watched her. A sense of numbness overwhelmed me. I suppressed an impulse to ask her about her "concept," figuring she'd tell me when and if she wished. While a creation by her own hands, it also felt unnervingly indifferent—*lifeless*—even as it grew, expanded. I wanted—and yet didn't want—to leave.

An hour later, out on Main Street, I still felt the claustrophobia of Jasmin's creation. It felt like something abandoned . . . even dead, with only a fossil of sorts remaining. Before I left, Jasmin invited me to come back and help her sculpt. I knew my curiosity, along with my confusion, would draw me back.

The experience brought to mind one of your recent pieces: the kinetic mobile of a human face you made in art class, with its echoes of artist Alexander Calder. The eyes, nose, mouth, forehead, and chin floated separately on wires. They'd come together, part, then join again. Like Jasmin's piece, yours disoriented me since the face kept bobbing into new configurations. Like the Gihon, your sculpture was constantly in flux. So are you. Recently, you took a pair of scissors to your own hair and cut it short, then bleached the bottom sections. It now kinks into a lovely, unconventional look that blends with your black, army-style boots.

We've talked about how it's hard for teenagers—indeed, for any of us at whatever age—to be unique unto ourselves while attempting to "fit into" groups. This is even more difficult as Separation ever more subtly tentacles us, try as we might to touch the aquifer's life force within us. Similar to your ingenious sculpture, your new style, and evolving character as somebody untethered to groupthink strains your fit within the ninth-grade subculture that you've helped create: *las cumpas*, or "the pals."

From what I gather from our chats, your group of friends has emerged in positive defiance to what's known in your Bolivian high school as the "mean popular girls," a clique in which members straighten their hair, self-brand with corporate logos, and date boys in upper grades. *Las cumpas,* in contrast, is a looser circle of a dozen girls. You don't necessarily flatten your hair or wear prescribed fashions. Though your group is also "popular" and extroverted, none of *las cumpas* dates yet. You have also helped shape *las cumpas* through the contrarian tone of your planned *quinceañeras*—you'd like to have one gathering in Santa Cruz and another in Samaipata—and they are to be simple, fun fiestas instead of lavish ones focused on social status and ostentatious display.

That's wonderful. But, as you've discovered, even the more unconventional cumpas space isn't "safe." I know it hurts when the very subculture you helped create begins to subtly reject you.

You've drawn looks from some *cumpas*, partly because of your new hairstyles but more because of the way you resonate with other groups, socializing with so-called "misfits" and new students. You've also resisted peer pressure to always socialize with las cumpas . . . or anyone else for that matter. Instead, during a recent two-week stint, you chose to spend each recess alone, going to the art room to riff on a piece. Think of how your self-confident, introverted retreat to the art room might cause other ninth graders, some of whom believe that teenagers are about only friends and pecking order, to reexamine their priorities. Though I gather many admire you as a leader, others question whether you're suitable for *las cumpas*.

The kids questioning you now are, yes, rebels enough to turn away from the "mean populars," but not quite enough to question the deeper "tracked" path you're all on. As *las cumpas* enter tenth grade, most of your parents and teachers subconsciously accept a Separated imagined order, viewing a high schooler's primary role as sociovocational: nailing the standardized exam you'll take at the end of next year, the results of which determine the bumper sticker on the back of the car. I'm aware of this perspective, and not just because it's so obvious in the *other* parents. I've had it branded into me: the two hundred thousand commercials, the high school teachers pressuring us, Long Island suburban culture.

Though I want you to be free in the deeper way we're talking about, I found myself, not long ago, encouraging you to do extracurriculars with an eye toward college scholarships. I caught myself afterward, but I suggested it because I know we don't have the means to pay full tuition for increasingly expensive US private colleges. And, like other parents, I want you to have the chance to do what your heart desires within society even as I know, more fundamentally, that we must create beyond its boundaries. So, as we adults ramp up various forms of tracking pressure on you and the other *cumpas*, peer gravity within your group invisibly reinforces this dimension of Separation.

My studio at VSC is housed in a two-story building called Maverick Studios. VSC gave me the "Henry David Thoreau" room, with the 19th-century nonconformist naturalist's name emblazoned on my pine door. I learned this morning the root of the word "maverick" when, as I've done each day since arriving, I stepped into the building's foyer.

Breathing in the building's now-familiar spring dampness, I noticed for the first time a framed page hanging on a far wall.

The page explained the origin of the building's name and gave this dictionary definition: "*maverick* (n): 1. an unorthodox or independent-minded person, 2. originally: an unbranded calf or yearling." A paragraph explained that the great-grandfather of Vermont Studio Center cofounder Louise von Weise was Samuel A. Maverick (1803–70), a Texas rancher who didn't brand his cattle, instead allowing them to run unmarked. Today's term "maverick" comes from Louise's great-grandfather's refusal to brand.

I think of you, two years back, when you performed scenes from the musical *Into the Woods*. I sat in the third row with Melissa and Clea in a downtown Santa Cruz theater as you sang a stirring "Giants in the Sky." You later told me you felt the music inhabit you. This is part of being maverick. It's what Jon meant when he talked about art: When you're a maverick, there is *nobody* in the room. Not even you. Certainly not a somebody with his or her own schtick, somebody with a quirky, but still Separation-embedded, personality. At its core, art is natural existence creating more of itself. It is river being river. It's Jasmin doing what artists do: revealing the life force by bringing into our presence something mysterious and even uncomfortable.

Consider von Weise, the great-granddaughter of the original Maverick. In the estuary of her seventies now, she and Jon have shaped a half-century along the Gihon River. Over the years the pair of wisdom keepers has provided thousands of artists a square inch beyond Separation. At the same time VSC has contributed to the economy of the lively, nonconforming Transition community of Johnson. Today, when I gazed down Johnson's Main Street, I was amazed to see its resemblance to Samaipata's Calle Bolivar. Johnson's Studio Arts and Crafts is Doña Anez' craft supply shop. Johnson's Main Street Brewery and Pub is Samaipata's La Boheme. Ebenezer Books parallels the itinerant bookstall on our Bolivian town's plaza. This Vermont town's weekly farmers market carries the same underlying essence as our daily *mercado*. Almost all of the hundreds of businesses in Johnson and Samaipata alike are uniquely imagined and owner run. Though externally different and five-thousand miles apart, the two Transition Towns share a core blend of individual freedom and close community.

Jon and Louise have been doing for decades what you've begun doing as you pioneer *las cumpas*—and whatever will evolve beyond that group. You've been, in a sense, coming of age outside of lockstep compliance to social norms. This is what I sometimes call being "maladjusted to empire." To use the image from the sculpture you made, when a person feels his face splitting apart and is not sure where he fits in, that's the precise moment to deepen into one's still, small voice the way you've been doing through your recess art retreats.

When it's friends we crave, it may seem illogical to go inward. But self-love and inner peace are the tributaries of deeper community. When one's felt identity of natural existence bursts out into relationship with the world in a manner free from Separation—that's maverick.

Today I visited Jasmin and discovered a huge change. The artist was closing in the only entrance to her studio.

I had to squeeze in sideways. Inside, the imminent enclosure felt oppressive. I waited until Jasmin took a break, and eventually she nodded over to the interlaced bamboo and some papier mâché.

I spent the morning, mostly in silence, working with her to—it appeared—eventually *block the only way in or out of her studio*. I wondered which side she planned to be on when she sealed it. Then I gazed out the window over Johnson's Main

Street: Wicked Wings Bar, the laundromat, and a Chinese restaurant. A twenty-five-foot freefall would preclude any window escape. And the window of her tiny bathroom was impassibly narrow.

The cool material wet on my hands, I mounted a stepladder and began wedging the plaster between bamboo strips. Jasmin was playing jazz, and the two of us worked without speaking. At one point she read from Ta-Nehisi Coates' *Between the World and Me*: "The people who could author the mechanized death of our ghettos, the mass rape of private prisons, then engineer their own forgetting, must inevitably plunder much more. This is not a belief in prophecy but in the seductiveness of cheap gasoline."

Jasmin turned the page and continued: "Once, the Dream's parameters were caged by technology and by the limits of horsepower and wind. But the Dreamers have improved themselves, and the damming of seas for voltage, the extraction of coal, the transmuting of oil into food, have enabled an expansion in plunder with no known precedent."

I stopped plastering to let this seep in. After a moment, Jasmin said that her creation had grown out of those passages as she searched for a way to represent visually how plunder of the Black body has become a brutal sacking of our larger body: the earth itself. And now the mystery began to come together for me. She had called it "a reef," and it dawned on me now why I had felt so uneasy, almost soul-sapped as I inhabited her sculpture.

As I got back to plastering, I remembered another reef.

It was in the Caribbean, off of the Honduran coast. Not long after college, a friend and I snorkeled there with a Krio fisherman guide who was eager to show us something significant. When we arrived at the reef it was obviously dead, bleached an eerie white by climate change. The reef no longer lived, he explained, but *creatures continued to inhabit it*, their colorful bodies especially bright against the bleached coral.

As we watched, parrot fish crashed into it and jellyfish and dinoflagellates lit it up with a magical glow of bioluminescence.
The reef was no longer a living coral system, but it did provide security and habitat. It was known and safe, so creatures
continued to decorate the inert object with their colors.

As I thought, Jasmin began to mumble. Then her voice
rose, and she began haranguing her sculpture: "We *all* consume a hundred times as much as any other animal, and we
all 'transmute oil into food, and plunder with no known precedent'! Black and white, women and men, same plunder. Gay
and straight, liberal and conservative . . . we *all* plunder. You
don't see any bears or chimpanzees or whales killing coral."

With pliers, she fastened a colorful plastic bauble onto the
sculpture. The color against the deadness reminded me of
those dinoflagellates lighting up the Honduran reef. Jasmin
continued: "We bicker over how to divide up the loot and the
power among ourselves, and forget we robbed the damn thing
and are gluttonously destroying it. At this rate, it'll be gone
soon—and so will we." She yanked back some chicken wire
and hurriedly wired a crimson red trinket to it. "Do we even
deserve to be here?"

I stretched to tippy toes to slap material onto the section I
was completing and felt something stir within.

I washed my hands in Jasmin's bathroom sink and
told her I had to go: the need to be alone suddenly felt
overwhelming.

Hustling across Mill House Bridge, I walked to a steep
waterfall along the upper reaches of the Gihon. Jasmin was
embellishing with flamboyant plastic scraps something that
was no longer there. Something life had vacated. More than a
metaphor for "Separation," her Reef is the powerful physicali-
ty of our speciesist imagined order.

Jasmin's Reef was the all of it: the superhighways and air-
ports, the GMO feedlots and biofuel power plants, the nuclear
missiles and prototype human brain chips. The Reef was what

the external world feels, smells, sounds, tastes, and looks like when enough of us believe "the Dream."

Maple leaves fell, one by one, into the pool beneath the falls before me. They were immediately drowned by the churning water. As I watched the leaves perform underwater flips, I remembered—with melancholy now—how your face lit up the other day when your *tía* invited you to live with them for a time on their land in Vermont. For all of their positive efforts, your *tíos*' Transition family is fragile. Even as they skillfully flow past Separation—and at times undermine it through creative community-building—they still, out of necessity, inhabit the Reef. They've hinted that it's a constant struggle. In America, pressure from advertising and from other families to "focus on the furniture"—that is, to update to more expensive sofas, appliances, and other material trappings—is ceaseless, and the B-word is in constant use ("I've been so *busy*"), including by those around your *tíos* who tend to overwork themselves and overschedule their kids. Similarly, Melissa and I have seen old friends lose, over the years, their one square inch of silence. It's become normalized, the way the dominant culture feeds on Mind and cultivates Separation.

Amaya, even as I feel inspired by the ripples sent forth by the thousands of communities re-tribing and fostering local economy, I'm reminded not to feel Pollyannaish about it. That's because all of this positivity can be smashed. Even as we recover what is good in life, we remain aware that it can be taken away through land grabs and global warming, biological warfare, and the way infotech and biotech are slipping into our organic bodies.

That's not to say we're to give up. It reminds me of when you were little and would scrape your knee or want to give up on the long climb up the mountain behind our house. I'd say the same thing to you that I tell Clea these days: "You can handle it because you're strong. You're a *Powers*."

Though I was referring to our family name, I really meant: *Humans are strong.* Though we're not magicians clever enough to bring a dead Reef back to life, we can do "hard." We were imaginative enough to come up with the fiction of a Separated social order. And we were diligent enough to spend generations building out a material "Reef" to serve this narrative of human supremacy. With a shift in consciousness, we humans are certainly creative enough to imagine a kinder social order and then—also over generations—rebuild a material order with respect toward the broad community of life. We do this work by braving even the parts of the river journey that surprise us with Class-Five rapids: IMPOSSIBLE TO PASS.

Twelve

This is Water

Hija,

Today the sky blackens above the Gihon. The National Weather Service warns of a torrent on the way, the one your *tío* mentioned during my visit: the *third* "hundred-year" storm this decade on a Separated planet in climate crisis. I walk along the Gihon's banks, on the way to the wider Lamoille River that it feeds. The Gihon winds through town, and I detour onto Main Street, recalling a dream from last night about a knife. Its ironwood handle felt heavy in my hand. When I awoke, I was still half-dreaming this was a blacksmiths' residency and that I was here to forge.

As my dream memory dissipates, I pass the Chinese joint and Ebenezer Books. A man with long dreadlocks on a porch picks an acoustic guitar; a woman in a minivan feeds the library book drop. When I arrive at the Lamoille riverbank, I find a couple of guys, one thirtyish and the other an old-timer, listening to rock music and drinking morning beers beneath an American flag at the Paradise Apartments. Laughing, they drain their cans and return to hoisting sandbags to protect Paradise from the forecasted floods. I linger on the bridge, watching them work to the music, and they notice me. I wave and muster: "Need help?"

Together they heave a sandbag onto the bank, and the older man laughs. "Why not?" he calls out.

We fill and move sandbags as the short, gray-haired Terry, says: "A doozy, this one's gonna be. We never used to get hit so bad."

These men are neighbors at the low-income Paradise, and they are attempting to protect their first-story apartments, in which they live as tenants, Terry on Social Security and the younger guy, Jeff, on unemployment.

When we break, I'm covered in sweat. I accept a can of beer, and Jeff turns up the music, Bruce Springsteen's "Thunder Road," and we gaze together over the white sandbags at the river as the sky growls.

After some hours of honest labor, I say goodbye and walk down to the Lamoille and up her bank, climate disruption forcing these new friends to spend their day barricading from a possible flood and causing me to think about how—even in a remote artists' residency—you can't hide from climate chaos.

A global storm is coming, but how to barricade ourselves from it? As a Reef calcifies around us and walls us in, how are we, and Gaia—the name we give the earth as an organism unto itself—to survive this?

The consciousness we cultivate now ripples through time. Take a few moments to remember the future. Float downriver to a possible projection of today's Separation. Imagine one of your great-grandkids–let's call her Gaia, after our own earth–a hundred years from today.

Gaia lives in one possible world, where hundreds of currently coastal cities are submerged, where diseases more lethal than Covid spread among species like wildfire and ravish the last vestiges of what humans used to call nature, and where your descendants live solely indoors, communicating through a kind of cerebral Wi-Fi as cell-phone technology, over decades, became chipped into our species. This world is run by a global elite whose bloodstream contains smart liquids to endow them with brainpower thousands of times that of humans. They control the bravest of new worlds through algorithms that keep their info- and biotech-boosted underlings undefiant. There she is: nine-year-old Gaia, *your own offspring and mine*, in a room where all windows are screens. She's unrebelling, arguably safe, and possibly content. But is Gaia human? How might we remember her differently?

At lunch, I sit at a Mill House table with Jasmin and a few other artists and poets, and we intermittently glance out the windows into the building rain. The predicted superstorm is starting. Verity Long, a thirty-two-year-old resident poet says: "Can you believe I'm still haunted by the words of David Foster Wallace from so many years ago? I graduated Kenyon College in 2005 and he gave the best commencement address I know of."

The waterfall beside Mill House thrums louder than I've ever heard it. Jasmin raises both eyebrows in Verity's direction as I allow this to settle. David Foster Wallace. Author of *Infinite Jest*. Committed suicide at age forty-six in September 2008 by hanging himself from a patio-roof rafter in the backyard of his southern California home.

"What Foster Wallace told us that morning was too amazing to summarize. But he started his speech with a parable about two young fish swimming along who meet an older fish swimming the other way.

Verity pushes back a stray lock of her long, dirty-blonde hair, her pale blue eyes mirroring the falls' rush. Then she recounts the fish parable I shared earlier.

Later, the rain temporarily abating to a grey sprinkle, I stream Foster Wallace's Kenyon speech in my attic bedroom. No video of the occasion is found online, but I do find a grainy audio of the speech which plays beneath a still photo of the handsome author, a bandana holding back his shoulder-length locks. I imagine you and me sitting together among that audience, absorbing his words—simple and clear, yet revolutionary.

He tells a younger Verity and the thousand other graduates seated before him that after college they will feel a fierce undertow of competitiveness. They'll become overworked. There will also be numbing "traffic jams and crowded aisles and long checkout lines," and over time their natural senses, thoughts, and feelings will stymie. It's a fierce struggle, he says, to stay within reality as corporations and governments "grow colonies in your heads."

I click PAUSE, and watch the rain, these words at once clear and mysterious, something vital in the deepest waters. I begin to imagine our individual head-colonies fused together into a hard coral Reef. I think of the outwardly successful David Foster Wallace hanging himself and wonder how that death relates to the Reef.

His words touch me, *hija*, and not just because of his celebrity status or the intrigue surrounding his suicide. Foster Wallace reaches into a space few have articulated. At one point in the talk, he says that our ingrained habits of thinking and doing are "a form of worship," and writes:

> [T]he insidious thing about these forms of worship, is not that they're evil or sinful. It is that they are unconscious. They

are default settings. They're the kind of worship you just gradually slip into, day after day . . . without ever being fully aware that that's what you're doing. And the world will not discourage you from operating on your default settings because the world of men and money and power hums along quite nicely on the fuel of fear and contempt and frustration and craving and on the worship of self. Our own present culture has harnessed these forces in ways that have yielded extraordinary wealth and comfort and personal freedom. The freedom to be lords of our own tiny skull-sized kingdoms, alone at the center of all creation.

Something else, wise and tortured, that Wallace left behind:

The capital-T Truth is about life *before* death. It is about making it to thirty, or maybe fifty, without wanting to shoot yourself in the head. It is about simple awareness—awareness of what is so real and essential, so hidden in plain sight all around us, that we have to keep reminding ourselves, over and over: "This is water, this is water."

After expressing it all so eloquently that morning in Ohio, why did David Foster Wallace later take his own life? His family and friends have reported what certainly appeared to be his lifelong struggle with biochemical depression and the varying, sometimes unpredictable, levels of relief he found through medication over the years. His case also highlights the complexity of our human existence in an increasingly Separated world—especially for those who, in addition to or because of experiencing mental illness, might be built to be society's "canaries in the coal mine," those who are somehow more sensitive, intuitive, and more maladjusted to being human in the Reef. Foster Wallace's own journals suggest he was, in fact, too sensitive for a world where the Tasmanian tiger, Steller's sea cow, and black rhinoceros have been crushed to extinction. A world where a Progress-addiction ended up killing 90 percent of Native people in what is now US territory.

I think of my student Kaitlin's peers at their town's train tracks. I think of you. How can I guide you toward—and offer practical tools to continue nurturing—an understanding of what is truly human, of biophilia? In further awakening this in you, how might I help you move not toward despair but toward a tenderness for the preciousness of your own and others' lives that lets you *live*?

How hard it has become for you and the rest of today's teenagers to be what you are: creatures in a territory to which you belong. Every morning, your school bus passes a hundred billboards flashing the things you must possess. At school— even as you try to mitigate it within *las cumpas*—you have to compete against Separation-programmed kids for grades and teacher praise, few around you aware that their world is imagined. On social media, you are an algorithm into which robots drop baited hooks. In short, you are informed that you are something make-believe and then further informed that that "something" is, by definition, never good enough. This is captured tersely by one major US corporation's motto: NEVER STOP IMPROVING.

Today's chiefs of industry use their considerable economic and media power to convince you and the rest of *las cumpas*, daily, to further Separate. Tesla CEO, Elon Musk, speaks from Separation when he says that building a city on Mars is "the critical thing for maximizing the life of humanity," while "thirty layers of tunnels" will relieve congestion in Earth's high-density cities.

Daddy,

This is water. *I'm going to write that on my bedroom wall.*

Thank you for sharing about David Foster Wallace. I listened to the speech, and it's beyond incredible. I also appreciate your trusting me, treating me like a mature person when we talk and in these letters.

*Today I remembered how you always pour a bit of your own drink into the ground—*para la Pachamama—*before saying "cheers," a tradition you picked up over the years in Bolivia. The love and respect indigenous communities give toward Mother Earth was passed to me generationally, through my mom and you. Having a connection to nature guides me away from Separation.*

Sometimes, at the end of certain days, I start to think doom thoughts too. So I bike around my neighborhood in Santa Cruz and look around. It makes me feel calmer.

As I bike, the world begins to vibrate peacefully as if it knew I was temporarily lost and that I needed it to be calm around me. The buildings are patient, and the birds remind me to look up and see the sun. This is water.

A red-alert text arrives today to all Vermont cell phones: "Imminent severe weather—flash-flood extreme warning in this area. Avoid flood areas. NWS." It's whispered that what's

coming is another Frankenstorm, a term coined by a journalist after Hurricane Sandy that refers to a hyperstorm exacerbated by industrial, heat-trapping gases released into the
atmosphere. A few years back, one of these newfangled tem-
pests killed dozens of people in this area and caused billions
of dollars in infrastructure harm.

I recall Hurricane Sandy in 2012, slamming the New York
apartment Melissa and I shared shortly before we moved to
Bolivia full time to be near you. Our workplaces—the United
Nations headquarters for Melissa, and NYU for me—shut
down for weeks. We were out of the city when Sandy landed,
and a friend said to me over a staticky phone line: "My
apartment is flooded out, the elevators don't work, there's no
power." His voice went fuzzy, and then I heard him saying,
". . . everybody's walking around like zombies on Sixth
Avenue, and the subways are drowned . . ." When Melissa and
I eventually made it back to our cold Manhattan apartment,
a stench walloped us when we opened the refrigerator. Our
building had gone almost a fortnight without electricity, and
all our food was rotten.

Today, I walk down to the Paradise Apartments and find
the sandbags in place, Terry and Jeff nowhere in sight. I'm
trying—failing, actually—to follow your wisdom, of *looking*
and appreciating the now. And though I'm so grateful for
your reminders, as I look over the Mill House Bridge, I
think only of the trillions of dollars in property destruction
caused by Sandy and Katrina, Harvey and Irma, and I
wonder—not just about the soundness of this single bridge
here in Johnson—but about the world's ability, in the coming
decades, to absorb the costs of climate mayhem unleashed by
an unchecked species.

I also wonder about the soundness of our psyches to
withstand another kind of Frankenstorm, the one released
into our cells. The coming inner Frankenstorm may not
feel so threatening. This parallel current flows softly in the

subtle form of algorithms created by the aggregate data generated over years of our device-recorded behavior. These algorithms, more and more each passing year, decide *for us.* Every time we search for music or movies, or ask a question to ChatGPT as if it were a friend or therapist, our personal cloud of data, and what's perfect to market into you, increasingly decides.

The robots of the future are unlikely to be the terrifying killers of most science fiction. They might, rather, be more sophisticated versions of ones existing today, like the Japanese-made "HRP-4C" female robot who looks, feels, and acts human. As we warm to her sadly beautiful eyes, HRP-4C's slight chest movements make us feel she breathes. Such devices could serve our unconscious instincts and cravings better than our partners or ourselves ever could do. How? By reading our complex algorithms and therefore "knowing" us better than any human could. Companies are now piloting almost unimaginable video-music-entertainment bots which release mood-appropriate scents and even massage us in whatever way we wish on a given day. Their HRP-4C-style seductiveness comes from how they process our biometrics. As they breathe and gaze at us, they also curate music, images, and caresses adapted to our changing moods.

With this in mind, *hija*, let's flow downriver again into the "estuary" of our own progeny. In this memory your great-granddaughter, Gaia, is somewhat older, and now no longer passive within a windowless room.

Gaia is alone on the moonlit deck of a ship. She's no flamboyant Lara Croft or Black Widow in her ordinary shorts, flip flops, and T-shirt, but she nonetheless conveys a superheroine's strength. The others on the ship—her community—dine below deck on what meager rations they have—this is a repurposed cruise ship retrofitted as a stealth ecovillage, but she's forgone the meal and

feels hungry as she gazes out over the ocean toward the scorched land.

Gaia knows. Knows that, in her great-grandma's lifetime, Earth lost an acre of rainforest every two minutes, knows that her ancestors overconsumed as biodiversity contracted along with felled forests. She knows that sea ice to the north and south melted, causing both oceanic and atmospheric feedback cycles as the darker melted areas absorbed yet more warmth and accelerated the warming that killed off what she'd heard was known as "coral." She knows that the merging of brain-computer interfaces and smart fluids into human tissues succeeded, and that now she is one of the last of the rebels, the un-enhanced. And she knows she and others are now under Elimination orders.

She knows, but is undaunted. The wind blows hard and it gets colder, but Gaia is scaffolded by the elements. She feels calcium in her bones, exploded stars in her plasma, and the water which composes most of her body. She feels herself as the reality of wild, pure existence.

Do you remember, over a decade ago, when Melissa and I picked you up in Santa Cruz and took you for a vacation visit to Samaipata, where we discovered a beautiful piece of land for sale? At that time, Melissa and I were newlyweds, and Clea was yet to arrive. How the three of us adored those five acres of rolling hillside, a tadpole-filled creek, and a grove of wild guapurú fruit trees, whose tangy-sweet purple fruits grow out of their velvety trunks.

You spent hours with us, joyfully walking the land. "It feels like we're in the country," Melissa said from the property's main hillock. "And yet that's the town-center, a stroll away." I gazed out over Samaipata's clay roofs and white façades, the green hills cupping it and framing a scene that could have been Tuscany if not for the sparks of green and red parrots flaring over our heads. Strong notes from mariachi trumpets drifted upward from a wedding somewhere below, and I caught the invigorating scent of eucalyptus.

A breeze rustled the yellow-flowering carnival tree overhead as you swung from its branches, yellow petals snowing down. From up in the tree, you confidently pointed out where "our house" would be. I noticed the joy you exuded by inserting yourself in that *our*.

I felt the joy in your words, too, and I imagined something that felt maverick to me at the time: We could ditch our jobs in New York City and build a custom adobe house on the very place at which you pointed. Couldn't we grow much of our own food on these acres—mandarins, pomegranates, bananas, vegetables of all sorts? What would stop us from reforesting the degraded flatter portions of it to create more habitat for the native guinea pigs and iguanas I heard rustling in the quiñe shrubs, and re-channeling the creek through the land to create fishponds? I imagined rising with the sun, working part time via laptop, and being so much closer to you, my first born.

Amid my musing, you climbed down from the carnival and began plucking purple guapurú fruit, popping the wild, grape-size morsels into your mouth. We followed your lead. The juice was warm on our cheeks. *This is water, this is water.*

IV

Estuary

Thirteen

Gaia's Seed

"What will Samaipata be like in a hundred years?" you asked last year under the guapurú tree on our hillock. We were reading together, and you'd just looked up from *Gone*, the science fiction book you were into.

I tented my book and considered your question. Beyond us I saw your persimmon tree, and Clea's peach, and below were the clay-roofed buildings of our town below.

"The future world," you said, replying to your own question in what I know as your anagram voice. "Towered, hurtful."

"Hey," I said, touching your shoulder. I tried to flip the energy with another anagram: "Don't forget we're in . . . the countryside > no city dust here."

We laughed, then threw some more wordplay and speculation back and forth. But later your anagram got me thinking more deeply about the future and who gets to shape it.

Shaping the future means power, and 80 percent of the world's wealth is controlled by just 10 percent of people. Humanity has long waged fierce class struggles to adjust such disparities, but the conflicts are usually about re-distribution within our own species and a given moment in history. How rarely we examine both how Earth's resources are shared not just among humans but within the community of life. It's those at "the bottom" of the imagined order and, often times, women—the Wangari Mathai's and the Kusi's and Indian Chipko treehuggers—who feel a deeper compassion toward Gaia, in part because ecofeminists empathize more deeply with the oppression of other species since they themselves have been oppressed by a Separated patriarchy. Especially in recent history, an elite class holding political, legal, educational, and media power gets to create and uphold the imagined order that shapes our present lives. And, most powerfully of all, this small group also sculpts the *future* into which our grandchildren will be born.

No, this is not a fantasy of Dr. Evil and the other nine rich people who secretly rule the world. We're talking about hundreds of millions of people, or around 10 percent of our species. The elite class is mostly centered in the Global North countries, not in Global South nations like Bolivia, a country which—for all its indigenous cultural wisdom and natural beauty—in important ways remains a natural resource-extraction colony for the rich. The imagined order keeps some 90 percent of the world's population cleanly on the margin of present-*and*-future-shaping. The select swath of humanity controlling nearly all material and political power is composed of diverse individuals who are mostly unaware that they exist within an imagined order that they themselves manifest and buttress each day.

A telling moment from a recent stateside trip Melissa and I took to visit our parents illustrates this: one evening in Boston, Melissa and I gathered with two of her college acquaintances and their spouses, three of the four of them Harvard and Boston University researchers. When the topic turned to super-intelligent computers and cyborgs, one of her former classmates praised the corner-coffee-shop robot barista who makes her morning cappuccinos, and her husband lauded Amazon for their new humanless stores where computers recognize your face upon entry and invisibly charge your account for any items you take.

I noticed Melissa flinch at all of this. Then Google's brain-chipping mission came up. The two couples felt unanimously positive about the project, with only a few slight caveats. "If my kid'll be a thousand times smarter," one said, "and there are no significant side effects, then bring on the surgeon."

Melissa shifted in her seat then, but we both kept mute. We sometimes find ourselves in top-ten-percent circles like this and know how thorny it can be to tread this kind of conversation. More than mere opinion leaders, the members of the upper-wealth tier are Mind-makers who receive astounding benefits from for-profit technology, so their allegiance to the Story of Separation tends to be lockstep and subconscious. In polite circles, patchwork critiques are fine—*bring down Putin, don't build a border wall, reduce corporate pollution*—but never question Progress. Probing Separation itself is sedition.

After a pause, Melissa wondered aloud about legislating limits on human enhancement.

The air in the room thickened as she spoke. Frowns began to form as the others realized she was interrogating brain-chipping. Then came nods, a "how-interesting!"—and a cheery topic switch.

Later, Melissa and I reflected on the exchange. Despite differing perspectives on Progress, we all had much in common. From kid challenges to aging parents to work, most other conversational topics turned out to be common ground. Melissa and I had the privilege of an upbringing and other factors that have helped us see and create beyond Separation, but we're *all*—from Wangari Mathai and Kusi to those researcher acquaintances to Elon Musk—molded, to one extent or another, by a speciesist imagined order.

If "water" is the natural life force we share, Separation is an artificial "oxygen" we breathe. I'm in the unusual position of calling out elite Mind-making power but not faulting anybody. The fault—or rather the dysfunction—*happened at an earlier point*, far predating, for example, those Boston folks' desire for chipped humans. It happened even before your great-grandfather told that Con Edison crew: "I'd rather have a light than a tree."

Again, we're visiting the Story of Separation, the deeper fissure between one species and its habitat.

That's why, in an attempt to comfort you, I can't try to airbrush over your suggestion that the future world will be towered and hurtful. After all, you, too, saw the newsclip forecasting that our meat will soon be in vitro, cloned, and raised in towers, those "AI-controlled vertical buildings" Google touts. And you're right that such towers are hurtful, and not just to the duplicated mammals inside.

Your anagram and your love of science fiction got me wondering how Separation—should it continue to remain invisible to most of us—might manifest a century downriver. What if your great-granddaughter, Gaia, lived in a very-possible world dominated by the same brain-chipped humans those Boston researchers and millions of others are now helping to create in direct and indirect ways? Today I send you from Vermont the first full installment of the life of your possible great-granddaughter, which grows out of the brief futuristic sketches of Gaia I sent you earlier. I'm glad you think it's a fun idea. Maybe you'll choose to edit or rewrite parts of it.

As you read, Amaya, just let things flow impressionistically. Think of this as another area where you and I might cocreate as we consider the future through fiction. When we project today's core dysfunction forward—when we futurize Separation—it's not to say that it will happen. I see it as a way to empathize with the *very real people who could someday live the consequences of what we do now.*

This empathy might even motivate us to ripple out future-sensitive trajectories. It's also very possible humanity could wake up and create a Transition-type future of a hundred-thousand energized local communities in harmony with the natural world. But this will only happen if we choose to slow our Separated course and tune into the life force. Should we do that, any number of beautiful worlds is possible!

Gaia's Seed

Chapter One: Fractures

June 21, 2129

Dear *Bisabuela,*

Calder and Julia splash together in the Gihon as I write to you from the riverbank. Every sunny summer day the pair of them swim, then sun themselves on Sugar Rock Candy Mountain, their name for their favorite Gihon-side boulder. Julia, at two, is so extroverted; the seven-year-old Calder, more reclusive. I'm gloomy these days—*La tristeza humana.*

Yesterday evening I walked, hoe in hand, on the clay road along our land's north-facing hill, the indigo clouds bordered in a cherry hue, and wondered if there was a specific moment when our community—Johnson, Vermont—started to fall apart. Was the tipping point a specific conversation between neighbors or lovers? Could it have been a specific Domain policy that started it? Or was something smaller still . . . like that cat-killed rabbit?

These were my thoughts yesterday, dear Great-grandmother, as the beech trees swayed. Beech gets a bad rap for sucking the ground dry, but how glorious their sound! I sliced hoe into earth, opening up an irrigation ditch I'd dammed a week before. It had been flooding our orchard, so I'd kept it dry for several days. The apples and peaches were overdue for a splash. I made a mental note to re-dam the ditch tomorrow because I've learned the peaches quickly overwater and shrivel.

As I then began work weeding the corn, Calder and our fourteen-year-old neighbor, Rachael, looked like dots on the other side of our sloping land. They were playing blackjack on our front porch–Calder's latest passion. In his carpentry workshop next to the house, my husband troweled some boards for our barn extension. Jim and I have been on a solstice technology sabbatical for the past three weeks. Gadgetless, we tend our farm, visit friends, and prepare vegetarian meals, centered *en familia,* tribe, and town. I'm amazed at the deep contentment I feel as Jim and I, exhausted, spoon in bed each night.

Anyway, while I was sweating away in the corn patch, Jim and Julia startled me with a close-up "*cooou*-ie!"– our family call. They'd crossed the orchard to see how I was doing. Rachael, who'd accompanied them, waved to me as she disappeared along our east footpath into town. Julia coaxed me away from my digging, tugging me down the hill to our pond. She immediately got naked and wanted me in there, too. Hot as I was, I obliged. Jim, too, was soon in habitat. Julia and I sang the water song: it's a never-the-same ditty about Mommy and Julia and the tadpoles she loves. We improvised, adding the names of our cats–Pachi and Boots–to the song this time.

On tech sabbaticals like this, I feel the deep time that our ancestors must have experienced. We don't rush, joining Pachi and Boots and the wild animals and the persimmon trees in their unhurriedness. As the sunset's cherry red loosened from sky, we dried off postswim, and ambled barefoot up to our dome-home because, as Julia cutely put it: "Me want food." But on the way back up, kitty Boots surprised us along the path with a headless baby grey rabbit in his mouth. Julia cried out, which got the dogs' attention. They came bounding through their range, chasing Boots and his rabbit prey into the blackberry thicket.

After dinner, a sleepy Julia said: "Boots is bad."

"Why?" I asked. I'd noticed Julia had been unusually quiet after seeing the dead rabbit in her cat's mouth.

"She . . . died, that *conejo*," said Julia, using the light Spanglish that had embedded in American English.

Calder, always wanting to be a man these days, repeated to his sister what he's heard Jim explain before: Boots kills rodents, like that rabbit, which would otherwise attract venomous snakes that could hurt us. "But . . . bunny died." Julia was choked up.

Jim hugged her. Then Julia asked, "We will die?"

The question—or was it a statement?—felt like a stabbing. We all went silent.

Through the window, the gloaming now. I spied Boots up an oak tree, and leaf-cutter ants stripped the jasmine vines climbing our portico in order to feast on their fragrant white flowers. "Yes," her Dad told Julia. "We'll die."

Courageous of Jim to say this to a two-year-old. It sounds improbable when everything is so *alive* with the rain, gardens thriving, the solstice-health we're all feeling, and Calder and Julia fresh as jasmine flowers. "Like everything else," my husband continued, hugging Julia, "we go back to Pachamama."

Can you hear me, *Bisabuela?* This letter to you began back in the Vermont Studio Center simulation, eight years ago, in 2121, as a way to retouch human language. After I crossed over the river, it became a diary of sorts. Yet how is it that I feel you're here, just inches away? I sense you listening to me and commiserating, so could it be that you are somehow reading this? Perhaps you are.

I never wrote to you about the first time I saw Jim, eight years back. He was on the far side of the Gihon, a few miles downstream from our farm. At first I thought it was a deer out there, but, as I stood to get a better look through my studio window, I noticed the creature stood on two legs. But it was something else. A fully organic human. A live Primitive.

The Primitive returned my glance for a few seconds then ducked back into the forest. But the same creature returned the next morning, remaining over there for a half-hour. I'll admit it, Great-grandma: I'd been tensely awaiting him, scanning the woods from my window. He approached to just a hundred feet away this time, diagonal across the Gihon.

The Primitive, who I would come to know as Jim, was chestnut-bearded with wavy, pushed-back hair and twinkling green eyes. Fit and muscled under a stained T-shirt, it wore jeans and sandals. It–*he*–looked a few years older than me, maybe thirty. When I opened my window for a better glimpse, a warm breeze rushed into my studio. I nodded to him.

He nodded back, never taking his eyes off me, then slipped into the forest.

It wasn't a total surprise to spot a Primitive. I knew from my pre-simulation briefing that by devolving, we risked contact. A group of us had decided to take a kind of experiential vacation away from our real life–as bracomi, short for "brain-computer interfaces." They are (I was) a thousand times smarter than humans. We were told that the Primitives might attempt poaching. We were forewarned that their villages had been pros-elytizing almost all of the seventy-five North America Domain simulations, figuring weirdos who chose to rough it as a writer, artist, or whatnot might be dis-posed to sedition.

What did surprise me, however, is that there'd be anything at the VSC simulation that was *better* than my previous life. I could not have possibly preferred any-thing to my 5D villa, the saturnalia orgies, and smallish other details like the end of work, boredom, and heart-break. Oh, and the end of diseases that made your 2020s Coronavirus look like seasonal allergies.

Your own Domain-happy, great-grand-'borg–yes, your quarter-Bolivian son, a well-known pre-Cusp semiotics professor from Philadelphia, is my DNA-grandfather, which makes you my *Bis*–could hardly have guessed she'd ever cross. But, after parking my nanodigestors, unmounting my chips, and stymying smart fluids, I end-ed up peering across a river and feeling . . . *lust*.

A week ago, *Bisabuela,* I was in the hammock when Jim approached and asked: "Can we talk?" This was not his usual conversational starter. I stiffened up.

"Umm . . ." he said, looking not at me but over the Gihon. "I'll just say it: I'm thinking of Bridging."

My tongue went inert. I'd never Bridge. Jim continued:

"It would mean two months in Maine. And I'd like to take Calder."

A long pause. I felt stunned. I couldn't imagine my own Jim, chipped and fluided up. Becoming bracomi, however altruistic the motive, carries huge unknowns and risks. "*Cuando*?" I asked.

"In a month."

"But what about *this*?" I said, getting up from the hammock, my arm sweeping out to encompass the land and community into which we'd so intentionally braided our family. I pressed fists into my own chest, but couldn't speak. I wanted to shout: "What about *human*?"

That evening, Rachael came over to babysit so Jim and I could attend a bonfire *despedida* get-together at our friend Mateo's a mile away. My hubby and I are communicators, but he'd hit my deepest pit of pain. So it was in silence that we walked along the dirt road to Mateo's, passing a group of two dozen Jehovah's Witnesses fanning out in pairs to distribute *Watchtower* magazines. A man in Sunday starch thrust a copy at Jim and invited us to "come talk about the Bible" at a weekly gathering. Flight patterns. Like the perennial summer migration of Deadheads through Johnson–our town is a point on their worn path between the Northeast Kingdom and Boston–so, too, do these missionary flocks alight in Johnson each year, leaving behind a few who, between migrations, occasionally flutter around and trill to passersby.

To the west of town, Jim and I passed the half-finished home of another Witness named Jesse. Viking-chic with his freckles, red hair, and a long, glowing, auburn beard, Jesse used to hunch over a laptop at Wicked Wings on Main Street, usually in a shockingly yellow polo shirt. Jesse lasted only a couple years in Johnson, having met, per one teller, "a beautiful Mexican girl, much younger than himself, and not a Witness." He abandoned the house, decamping with his fiancée "to Michigan or Illinois or perhaps..." The teller gestured vaguely to points west.

Still walking in what was for me an aching silence, Jim and I passed a compound of incongruity: four airy modern homes, each belonging to a different family of schismatic New Animists, descendants of bracomi-defectors from New York. Floor-to-ceiling glass walls and balconies faced the paradise view of the Green Mountains, the Gihon River sparkling below. The little clan possessed the rarity of a turquoise swimming pool and a private water supply in this parched fringe of town still unconnected to community lines. Sometimes I spotted them on dirt bikes, on the rare occasion they left their "*burbuja de Anamistas*"–their Animist bubble. In the meantime, a 24/7 'bot gardener keeps their properties green. In our DIY-town 'bots used to be taboo and "animism" meant something visceral that we all felt. It didn't need a name or a religion.

We looped around toward the Lamoille River, still in silence. I held Jim's hand, then couldn't stand the tenderness and let it drop to his side. I tried to recall the yearning that drew me to him...

After seeing Jim that first time across the river, back when I was still bracomi and conditioned to see him as "Primitive," I found myself breathless. I spent the rest of that day trying to distract myself in the Vermont Studio Center woodshop with "Gerald," a Type-A computer-geek program, year unidentified, who was contorting two-by-fours into curves with a bandsaw and dowels. To Kurt Cobain on a CD player, Gerald sandpapered his bent-wood magic, tutoring me on how to vise-grip segments together. But, trying in vain to forget the Primitive across the river, I couldn't focus on lumber, so Gerald kicked me out.

From Gerald's, I walked a Gihon-side path, suddenly tired of the VSC simulation mockup reminiscent of your era's Civil War or Medieval reenactments. I arrived at the Gihon-Lamoille juncture and decided to mix things up through a swim.

After backstroking for twenty minutes, I felt something warm rush out of me. *Pee.* Fully evolved bracomi–what I was before coming to the simulation and de-chipping– don't do that because nanodigestors excrete their waste through skin-pore vapors. But since I'd arrived in the sim, it seemed my body had regained the ability to excrete urine. Amazingly, that liquid still emerged from what was left of *my own* Primitive body, and it struck me that it was the same water I ignored as I whipped over streams and bays as a bracomi.

But treading water that day, I felt the Gihon all around me and realized my pee was now part of the three-hundred-million cubic miles of water circulating Earth as water, rain, vapor, snow, and hail. Could it be that I was synchronized not just to the planet but also to the sun and moon that cause the ocean's tidal flows and the tiny tides in my own, still-existing bladder?

That realization led to a mutinous thought: could the Domain be lying?

Our commonest refrain–*We are a thousand times smarter than Primitives*–was a fact, at least when it comes to sheer brain-power. But could it also be true that the unenhanced "Primitives" that everybody was in your time, dear Great-grandmother, can tap a vast acumen much greater than bracomi?

"Johnson's breaking up," Mateo said, at the bonfire later. Four of us were gathered: Mateo, Jim and I, and Thiago, a bachelor permaculture designer friend.

Jim hid his eyes from me, gazing out toward the rushing Lamoille beyond the firepit. Mateo hardly needed to elaborate. So many breakups. Our friends Anette and Thomas, homesteading organic farmers who make the local beer and juice we drink, were divorcing after nearly two decades together in Johnson. She was to take over their ten-acre farm outside town, and he'd build a house on a lot they own in town, with his new partner; their teenage son, who's just threatened–the ultimate teen rebellion–to go bracomi, would straddle these arrangements.

Mateo, who looked downcast in the bonfire glow, and his partner of eight years, Ivete, an acupuncturist of Brazilian descent, have also split. I remembered Mateo's gusto when I first visited his glass workshop. "As a bracomi," he told me in those days, "something was always missing. Here as human again I've repurposed myself." Now, two years later, his repurposed wine-bottle lamps shimmer inside our house, but he's shuttered the workshop.

I don't love you anymore. That's what he told Ivete, and it drove her into depression and out of Johnson. She passed her clay-based soap-making business on to a friend and moved to Maine, where she plans to practice her acupuncture in a coastal village. At her going-away party, she and I slow danced, but really it was Ivete holding on and hugging me as her tears fell on my arm and she blamed Mateo for doing this. She told me she wanted to stay in Johnson, and will return someday, but for now she needs to leave a place with so many memories. Up for sale: their sixteen acres, the half-built eco-house, a beat-up van, and their dog-eared copy of *Permaculture: A Designers' Manual*.

"I'm not sure what I'll do," Mateo tells us. "Illinois first, where I have a gig to earn twelve-hundred in ten days. And next . . . I mean, can anyone finish a sentence starting with 'And next' these days?"

Mateo got quiet, stared into the flames. He'd shed his partner, his business, and was now about to shed Jim and me too. If there was a lightness in this new "freedom" for him, it wasn't audible in his voice.

Thiago, meanwhile, munched coca leaves and recounted the magic of his fortnight at the permaculture and eco-village gathering in western Mass, enthusing over the droves of bracomi treasoning to our side. "We called it 'The Gathering of the Vibes' and ten-*thousand* people showed up, *hombre*, many of them recently devolved. They see through blinding by a billion pixels and want to rewild their ingenuity with us. *Sin duda*, the Domain could fall!"

Jim flashed an ironic look at Thiago. One I know well. "It'll take more than 'Vibes' to even dent the Domain."

What Jim didn't add is something we all know: a jittery Domain had just begun targeting our human towns.

It happened with the increase in bracomi urban mutinies as bracomis themselves question the Domain. Then came the mass defections from North American simulations —my own defection from the VSC simulation writ large. Last month, a forced re-volve policy for defectors was announced, and everybody in Johnson is wary. But Thiago, tipsy, insisted on a human future, as he told us news about rebel bracomis monkeywrenching the heart of the Domain. "This week alone they torched eight Flashports!" he said.

"Right," Jim said, "but things are stiffening into a police autocracy. The Domain has executed some of them as 'terrorist sympathizers.'"

I listened, still hurting, *Bisabuela*, as the men bantered over the fire. Mateo may be right, that despite all of this chaos, things could go our way. I mean, the reason defections from bracomi are so high is because of the more irresistible world *we humans* have been creating in thousands of local towns and villages. With zero inner-tech and the exact same biochemistry that people had in your day, a century ago, those of us outside the Domain's gates—and *inside* a newfound freedom—have learned to biomimic bacteria to create productive soils. We've reduced labor through hydrogen-powered everything, from tractors to dishwashers. We've upped lifespans and reduced infant mortality by bio-attuning to discover natural medicines which eliminate many of the diseases that your pharma-firms used to spend trillions on. (Remember the billions spent just on Covid vaccines in your time? And the billions more on booster shots?) And we've reduced conflict in our communities and discovered the sort of peace Calder, Julia, and Jim feel through community gardening, daily group meditation, and our evolving conflict-resolution practices.

So why are we fracturing? For starters: We've all been through the Climate Wars, and that trauma is in our bodies, our troubled marriages, and our de-tethering communities. Each day I do visualizations and take several actions I feel can help my community to avoid further splintering.

But I wonder, today, if I even did the right thing to give birth to Calder and Julia, bringing them into a world that's getting more dangerous each day. A world where even my own *husband* is about to Bridge. Should I have held in check my passion for Jim—and also, if I'm honest, an adventurer streak in me that urged me to 'go primi-tive'—and instead returned to the Domain after the VSC simulation?

No, *Bisabuela*. I couldn't have remained separated from my organic nature. Not after I gazed across the water and began to *feel*.

Fourteen

A Wisp of Soul
Carrying a Corpse

Dear Amaya,

Today the Gihon engulfs its banks. An uprooted beech tree catapults over the falls, end-over-ending into the rising flood. Wind shrieks. The forecast storm has arrived at VSC.

As water spanks the roof and whips my clerestory attic-bedroom window, my thoughts rush to Terry and Jeff in their poorly sited Paradise Apartments, its foundations low on an engorged Lamoille. I wonder if the sandbags I helped them pile up have held. On impulse, I head out to visit them.

But when I step out into the rain, it feels like bird shot. Nobody is out there in this stinging rain. I recall Jasmin beside her Reef sculpture reading from *Between the World and Me*. "The Earth's vengeance is not the fire in the cities but the fire in the sky." Might this be the Frankenstorm of which we'd been warned? The river heaving against the Mill House Bridge, I wonder if it will hold up under this surge.

Stranded in my room, I get a message from you:

> Daddy, I'm tingling after reading about our descendants. *Que* cool! Any of this could actually happen. But what's 'Bridging'? Weird suggestion: I have an idea about what happens next with Gaia. LOL. Send you ideas?

> That's not a 'weird suggestion' from an actress, artist, and storyteller like you. Send away!

Looking out my window into the torrent, I recall a hike you and I took two years ago in the wake of a hard rain, through the Bolivian hamlet of Piedras Blancas, on the edge of Amboro National Park. Do you remember how I surprised you by rerouting us off the main trail? We scampered down a soggy path leading into an old family cemetery half-overgrown with banana trees. You became silent when we arrived. One can't help but venerate such a place. Motioning to the gravesites, I said: "This is you someday." You flashed a smirk and exclaimed: "*Daddy!*"

But the moment stuck with you. A month later, I overheard you, in thoughtful tones, telling Clea and Melissa about it. I hadn't taken you to the cemetery to be morose but, rather, to affirm that our death is not to be hidden, feared, or overcome. It is one of our best gifts. Death is a key portal into the maverick ways your Vermont *tíos* and so many millions of others are undermining the imagined order today. Beneath dogma and creed—beneath Separation—exists an essential, daily way of connecting with fundamental reality that allows us to be fully ourselves, regardless of societal pressure toward conformity: remembering that we will die.

Considering death as our ally—even considering it at all—is countercultural. Many business executives and politicians race to re-engineer us *out* of death because, conditioned into

Separation, their biggest fear is the body's dissolution. They simultaneously try to hide death.

To fight death, our species is on an immortality quest. To give two examples of hundreds of current projects: geneticists have tripled the lifespan of the *Caenorhabdtitis elegans* worm, and nano-technicians are midway toward a bionic immune system featuring a million micro-robots to inhabit our mammalian tissue, barricade our blood vessels, and reverse aging.

To hide death, TV series and advertising provide fantasies of everlasting youth. Taboos are placed on meaningfully discussing death, and, at least in the US, great efforts are taken to hide it. Sick and aged people rarely stay in their home; they are whisked away to hospitals or nursing homes where the healthy and young won't have to engage with the process of advanced aging, sickness, and death. You can also see it in the way the US deprioritizes the Day of the Dead and other customs or rituals that honor our ancestors and remind us of our own fate.

One of many reasons I love Bolivia is its continuing connection with the reality of death. I appreciate the annual ritual each November 1 of walking to our town's cemetery and joining the somber-yet-festive celebration of those who have passed. And I appreciate knowing that your sister, as she walks to school, might pass the home-based wake where Don Manuel's coffin awaits the visit of friends and family. In Samaipata, the church's bell still tolls if someone in the community dies—a ready reminder that a soul has just been released back into the ether.

Sometimes I walk by the cemetery in our town and think about the lives of the people who rest there. The truth is, I talk to them as I go by. I see them as a little community. I think about their lives and the work they did. In the bigger picture, I know that I am headed there. Of course, I'd rather be alive right now than in their place. I love this precious, brief existence as a breathing mammal. But, whereas in the past I feared the dissolution of my body, I don't anymore. Indeed, much of what I've been sharing in these letters—about tapping biophilia and living in reality outside of Separation—connects to the power of a revised understanding of death.

Consider it this way: isn't it logical that the transient manifestation of your brain and your body is not *who you are*? When you die, only then do you go back into who you are. You return to what you have been for 99.99 percent of time: your self of "spiritual," or pure, existence. You have but for a brief moment been a body before returning to your true identity: existence itself. Or the life force.

When I fully absorbed this, *hija,* I felt incredible liberation. It's the freedom to de-tether from *all* imagined orders and "play" within an exquisite incarnation, knowing all along how fleeting it is. Instead of enacting a role within the fiction of Separation, why not *live* now? Living in one's beautiful bodily form—while it lasts—is about as far as it gets from being "born" merely to someday "die." With this consciousness, our lives are more akin to a river which cycles and transforms.

There is a powerful, simple practice you can do to access this deeper kind of freedom. It's called "Die before you die":

You might try it by simply lying down in a quiet place for ten or twenty minutes. Close your eyes. Feel your breath go in and out. Then imagine your next outbreath as your last.

Your heart stops. Remain there lying on your back—in the yoga posture called *savasana*, or corpse pose. Feel the life-energy drain out of your body, perhaps through the top of your head. You've died, but only bodily. You may sense how the life force contained in your body has rejoined an ocean that existed epochs before "you" manifested as a particular mammal, an

ocean that will be there for epochs to come.
Then, open your eyes. What a gift to remain in a
physical body, but with the consciousness of your
deeper identity of timeless natural existence.

It touched me, several years back, when your little sister said to me on our hillock above the fishpond: "When I die, Daddy, I want *Pachamama* to turn me into a flower. And you will be a petal in my flower."

Then Clea thought of you and said: "So will my sister." She added that Mommy will be another flower growing next to her, "a friend."

The wind soft in the tree leaves above, the air was fragrant with pine. After a pause she added: "But we don't decide what we are after we die. Pachamama decides."

Nobody told little Clea this story. It drifted out of her own awareness, out of the atmosphere in which she dwells. What your sister seemed to say—looking through five-year-old eyes—was that we humans are but one strand in an evolving earth. We die back into humus, into the sovereign life force from which we've come, and although Clea would like to believe that she, you, Mommy, and I will someday sway together in the wind, she knows that decision belongs to another.

You got quiet a couple years back, when I told you that your Giggi, my mom, had multiple myeloma, a cancer of the bone marrow.

We were sitting side by side on a public bus traversing a boulevard in Santa Cruz. You absorbed the news, then asked how far along she was, and I told you we didn't know yet. There would be tests . . . and, and. Later that day we called your Giggi, and, as in the other conversations I've had with her since the diagnosis, her voice shimmered with acceptance and joy. "Your Pop and I are living this new stage as an adventure," she said, "and it's beautiful to have someone beside me, my partner of fifty years."

After that, during our visit to Giggi and Pop at their North Carolina home—when you came with me on the speaking tour two years back—you swam with Giggi in her community's pool, and we went with her and Pop to a Lady Tar Heels basketball game. You'd known that they attend all the UNC women's basketball home games, but how different it was to be there in the crowd with them, wearing the light blue "Heels" cap Giggi got for you.

For me the most touching moment of the visit was a deeper exchange of gifts. You gave Giggi *Bolivianita* earrings, explaining to her that the purple gems are unique to your country. How the *Bolivianita* shone in the light streaming through the window into Giggi and Pop's prayer nook, where each morning and evening they read sacred words together, contemplating existence and sending out gratitude and prayers. Giggi took the earrings in her beautiful wrinkled hands and inserted them into her earlobes.

Then she said, "for my *nieta*"—granddaughter—and handed you a pendant in the form of a child, a symbol of you that Giggi has worn over her blouses since you were little. It's made the trip with her down to Bolivia to visit you each year, and now was the time to pass it on. With an amethyst gem for a body, your pendant has a gold wire head, legs, and arms.

You wear it as a necklace, and whenever I see it, I'm reminded of that moment when my mother and my daughter exchanged not just of the substance of Earth's stone but of something human and primal. Similar to the pendants she's worn for each of her five grandchildren, each one with a unique size, shape, and jewel, her gift to you seemed to take on the almost Neolithic shape of a child. It could have come from a cave painting or statuette, from a time when humanity blended with the life force—from an era of the universal "great mother" that ripples through us in contemporary times through the *Tao Te Ching* in the form of the generative feminine: mysterious, beyond birth and death.

A grandmother on her journey, in the estuary—nearly ocean—passes her *nieta* something from the source as she herself begins the river journey. I love my mother, deeply, and don't want her to go someday. But one of the gifts she's passed to me was shimmering right there in her voice as she peacefully shared her diagnosis: an acceptance of the flow of life.

Here in Vermont, VSC resident artists and writers occasionally gather in the evenings to share work. Last night, most of the fifty-plus of us in residence collected for a spoken-word performance, in part to mark the close of the fierce storm.

A few days had passed, and so had the tempest. Though punishing, it could have been worse. Mill House Bridge held, but another local overpass was destroyed. It's one I'd crossed several times on walks, a wooden bridge spanning a Gihon-side tributary which leads to a bubbling spring in the hills above. As I waded across the river in the place where the bridge had been smashed, I wondered some more about our progeny, Gaia, a hundred years from now. I wondered about the resilience of our species' bridge to the future.

At the performance, several poets and novelists shared their writing. The final author was a young man from India: Raghu Karnad. He walked slowly to the podium and opened his book, *The Farthest Field*, about Indian participation in World War II battlefields in Europe. Raghu's oval eyes gleamed in the spotlight as he read in a soft baritone voice: "Human beings have two deaths: the first at the end of their lives, when they go away, and the second at the end of the memory of their lives, when all who remember them are gone."

He paused. I noticed his tears about to break. "That second death," he continued, "is the farthest field."

When the readings ended, artists and writers rose and shuffled out into the night. I fell away from the group and walked alone along a Milky Way-ribboned Gihon, stopping below Jasmin's second story window to see the artist throwing papier mâché onto the expanding lifelessness of her piece. The reef now encrusted all but one corner of a studio nearly interred, as if the art space were fossilizing. Watching her, I wondered at rejoining "the farthest field." What does each of us choose to create during our brief lives? And how does the spirit we cultivate affect the world where our names and actions are, ultimately, forgotten?

The perspectives on death I share with you are not embraced within Separation. Remember how Melissa's Boston acquaintances felt fine with the prospect of chipping their kids? They also spoke against any limits onto the artificial extension of human lives. Similarly, one of my college friends, now an urban executive, said to me, "I thought we'd have figured that out by now." This was later on that same trip, and I'd been talking to him about the tension between my profound sadness over my mom's bone marrow cancer and my underlying acceptance of the transience of life.

"Figured out what?"

"*Death*," he said.

My friend, though being ironic, wasn't joking. This opinion is widespread, the idea that science and technology as usual will not just extend lifespans to, say 130, but that we'll be able to completely conquer death sooner or later. That friend of mine now has his first child in college. Melissa's colleagues' kids are growing toward bumper sticker terrain soon, too, and you'll be meeting them. Or others like them, if your plan to go to college in the States comes to be. Students like my undergraduates. Though you've tagged along on a few of the field trips in my "Bolivia: A Case Study in Sustainable Development" course, you've yet to experience how many American undergrads are conditioned into an elite-imagined orthodoxy.

It's not surprising that this is so. The majority of my private university students are the kids of top-ten-percent parents fused into an ideology of human supremacy which ultra-privileges them. But even the ones on scholarships, many of them students of color and working-class white students raised outside elite strata, also grew up within an imagined order promising social ascent through compliance to Story. And *death*, in the Story of Separation, is a decipherable problem.

To get a sense of the elite consensus around death, here's a rainy afternoon moment in my Samaipata classroom last year. Mid-discussion, I shared a line from a brilliant freed-slave philosopher: "Epictetus," I told the group of American twenty-year-old exchange students, "said that each of us is 'a wisp of soul carrying a corpse.'"

Curiosity infused the room, and I looked around the semicircle at students who attended schools like McCallister and Yale, Cornell and Tulane. The biggest concern for many of them, heading toward their senior year, was their first job after college. The second biggest topic was often whatever assignment was next in the docket and how they could leverage it toward maximizing their debut social-vocational niche.

I put the clicker down. "Epictetus is pointing out that each of you was dead for billions of years *before* you incarnated," I said. "Then you will also be dead for billions more after your heart stops."

Total silence. Fidgeting began. The general discomfort seemed to ask: *Can't we get back to debt-for-nature swaps and the Andean concept of "living well"? These topics stimulate without confusing me.* The students were experiencing "cognitive dissonance," a psychological state where—when faced with an insight that contradicts what we already believe—we resolve the tension by rejecting the new information to remain within the comfortable confines of present beliefs.

I sensed oodles of cognitive dissonance getting resolved just like that. After all, to actively consider what Epictetus was saying would mean questioning the central importance most of us place on an individualistic story of meaning and success. To let in thoughts of the shortness of life—and thereby stick a toe into the river of pure existence—could mean abandoning the known ego system.

Normally, the majority of students in a class like this instantly dismiss intrusions like Epictetus. Only three or four are open to it, and these mavericks tend to hail from unconventional families of varied social class and ethnicity where a deeper skepticism was instilled. Or else they experienced severe sidelining because of having been pushed to the margins of society for one reason or another—a deep crisis, in some cases, or marginalization because of the color of their skin or personal choices.

One young woman in this particular class possessed this kind of openness. Such a posture invites one of the more liberating emotions: confusion. If you're not confused, you're likely fused, as the saying goes. In this case, most of us are fused to the story that happiness means either ignoring the farthest field or striving to solve death. Why not, rather, allow ourselves to linger in the unknown, to allow confusion to flow unobstructed?

The student broke the silence by saying: "*This* is my biggest problem." Some nervous giggles, as the room exhaled.

"What is your biggest problem?" I finally asked.

"That I will be dead for billions of years." More giggles. Then she looked off into the distance through a classroom window. At last she added: "My biggest problem is that I'm 'a wisp of soul carrying a corpse.'"

Fifteen

Amor Fati

When I visited Jasmin this morning, I found her captive in the Reef.

I stooped to peer through a forehead-sized opening where the door had been. It was now bambooed and plastered over. Jasmin sat cross legged on the floor inside. I had an apple with me and passed it through the hole, the apple's red vibrant against the bleached-out Reef. As Jasmin stood to accept it, I asked her when—*if*—she planned to leave. And how?

The Gihon thrumming in the distance, Jasmin didn't answer. The lights were out in the room, and the only light came through the half of her window that was still unplastered and that filtered into the Reef through her bathroom door. She sat back down, munched her apple. I stood there for some ten minutes, at the entrance, no longer able to go in and help her. She rose and continued to fasten colorful baubles to the sculpture, to my surprise—*whistling* as she worked. She seemed, despite the outwardly dire circumstances . . . joyful.

After I left Jasmin's hallway and walked down to the Gihon, a strong memory surfaced: you were three, during the time when I was working in New York. Your mother came up with you from Bolivia, bringing you to Little Rock, Arkansas, to visit her host family from a US high school exchange year a decade back, and I flew out from New York to visit. You and I spent five beautiful days together.

On the last night before I returned to New York, I kissed your cheek and said your beautiful name aloud. "*Amaya.*"

Then you said mine. "*Papá.*"

"*Hija,*" I said.

"*Papá,*" you said. The moon waxed oblique. The trees tossed in the wind, and I felt warm and shivery at the same time.

"*Hija.*"

"*Papá.*"

"*Hija.*"

"Daddy," you said, switching languages. A plane crossed the moon, its tail of exhaust gray on the moon's white.

"Daughter."

"Daddy." You smiled and kissed me. I said your given name. You said *Daddy*, serious now. And I said yours. We were memorizing each other.

The next morning on my flight out, I rose above Little Rock, looking out over a tiny airport, those couple of skyscrapers enveloped by the big curve of the Arkansas River and all the soy-scarred land stretching north, and a part of me ached for the same thing I knew you did: to somehow be *en familia* with your mom so we could be together every day. But I knew it wasn't possible.

I think again of the time you anagrammed The meaning of life into The fine game of nil. In that moment, we skirted the edge of this sensitive topic. I sensed—underneath your bravery and positivity as an actress, artist, and leader—a vulnerability over growing up split between two households. The core of what I want to say to you about this is: *It's not your fault.* I think you know this logically, and I've said it in person, but do you really know it and feel it? Your mom and I came together, only to separate, and parts of us remain Separated in the larger sense—and none of this is your fault. Nor is it ours. It just *is*.

〜〜〜〜〜〜〜〜〜〜〜〜〜〜〜〜〜〜〜〜〜〜〜

Gaze out into the distance toward a high point, perhaps a tree or rooftop. I imagine sitting atop that perch, looking back at yourself in your actual location and situation.

Simply observe yourself feeling upset or perhaps judging a situation or person–whatever it is.
Then scan out over the area around and beyond, observing the thousands of other people, houses, and trees. How do you feel now, seeing yourself in this wider perspective?

〜〜〜〜〜〜〜〜〜〜〜〜〜〜〜〜〜〜〜〜〜〜〜

When I was about to turn fifteen, much in my life situation also seemed unfair, even distressing. Although I'd gotten over a humiliating childhood stutter, I was thin and gangly, and struggled for a place in the junior high school cliques. Also, at the time I sensed a growing tension between my parents. Into this mix, a wise teacher of mine taught me this visualization. I still do it from time to time:

This exercise helps me lessen emotional pain and stress by reducing my ego's reactivity. When I do it, I sense how *tiny* my body and brain are. They're interconnected within a pattern which, from this broader viewpoint, contains dozens of square miles. From the treetop I also intuit a larger entirety still: *billions* of people and trillions of other creatures within what is perhaps an infinite cosmos.

The decision to maintain inner peace no matter what happens may seem naïve or weak, but it's powerful rebellion. Instead of reacting to every little thing—or even to apparently *big* things like separated parents or Separated Frankenstorms—what if we instead considered this thought from a former slave: "Don't seek for everything to happen as you wish it would," Epictetus said, "but rather wish that everything happens as it does—then your life will flow well." Let's say something happens that you wish had not happened. Which is simplest to change: that event, which is past, or your opinion of the event? We acquiesce to what has happened by changing our wish that it had not happened. This Stoic practice is similar to the Buddhist's total acceptance of what is.

We can take this even a step further because we have the ability to not only *accept* what happens but to actually *enjoy* it—whatever it is.

Nietzsche used *amor fati* to capture this perspective. To wish for whatever happens to happen is a smart way to avoid disappointment because in that case nothing is contrary to your desires. But to actually feel gratitude for what happens? To love it? This is a path to joy.

Even zooming out just slightly, as we did in the treetop exercise, helps us to see ourselves within the web of life instead of trapped in the cage of ego. What happens to us as individuals may seem unfair . . . but only if we're caught up in labeling some particular manifestation of the life force as upsetting or cruel or inexplicable. Such events could, in fact, make perfect sense if viewed within broad ecology.

This process of shifting viewpoints does not happen automatically. It's an iterative practice. At fifty, I continue to stumble into dried-out loops of judgment, evaluation, and criticism, so I have to—on a daily basis—employ the sorts of perspectives and practices we've been discussing to reenter the animate waters of acceptance, forgiveness, and positive action. I like how spiritual teacher Ram Dass summed this up, in a talk late in his life. It's a humorous summation of the fruits of an *amor fati* spiritual path.

"I was trained as a psychologist and in analysis for many years," Ram Dass told the audience. "I taught Freudian theory and was a therapist. I took psychedelic drugs for six years intensively. I have a guru. I have meditated regularly since 1970. I have taught yoga and studied Sufism and many kinds of Buddhism. In all that time, I have not gotten rid of one neurosis." Here he paused, to laughter, then added: "*Not one*. The only thing that's changed is, whereas previously those neuroses were these huge monsters—'Oh no, don't take me over again!'—now they're these little shmoos. As in: 'Oh, hi there 'Shop-My-Way-to-Happiness.' I haven't seen you in days, come in and have some tea.'"

After those rough pandemic years, many of your classmates might feel resistant to an *amor fati* perspective. After all, where is the line drawn? When do we practice *loving what is*, and when do we make other decisions, like starting an alternative-high-school subculture or a Transition town? For me, it's become a question of acting out of acceptance and love instead of *re*-acting out of fear and blame. It's not easy, but I try to accept—entirely—what's beyond my control, no matter how difficult it seems. And I also choose to love it. After all, *it's there*, so by definition it has already happened and can't be undone. More than that, the past is insubstantial. It exists within us only in the way we choose to harbor it.

For example, I recall a particularly hard day during the pandemic. Melissa and I had just had one of our worst arguments in a long time. Clea felt our stress, and you, too, were at a low point, burdened by a year cooped up inside and taking online classes. I was about to further defend my point of view to Melissa—digging a deeper trench of ego—when I saw a rainbow in a sliver of broken glass.

A water pitcher had fallen over the previous day and fissured. Now it sat there on the kitchen table, flashing a polychromatic wink at me. I immediately woke up. I excused myself and went out for a walk. Although my Separated mind megaphoned an internal dialogue about how "right" I was in the argument, a calmer, long-honed voice in me began what's become habitual: flipping negativity into mindfulness. That day, instead of going more deeply into the mire, I looked at my inner turmoil and asked: *What is this?* I became curious about my pain instead of critical of myself and others. Meanwhile, walking in fresh air was already lifting my spirits, and, after a while, I noticed the creek flowing by my feet, bringing to mind some lines from the *Tao Te Ching*:

Nothing in the world is softer and weaker than water.
Yet, to overcome the hard and strong,
Nothing surpasses it.
The weak overcomes the strong.
The soft overcomes the hard.

The ever-available softness and beauty began to wash away my inner rigidity. How grateful I felt that Melissa and I were imperfect humans! Thankfully, we'd yet to brain-chip or smart-fluid ourselves into some kind of unnatural "perfection" where we never disagreed. I began to feel gratitude for how I regularly lose the way, because that's what reminds me of a human's natural ability to access tools like meditation, mindfulness, and *amor fati*.

I went back inside and apologized to Melissa for losing my temper. I also reached out to both you girls, catching up on tadpole updates from Clea and then listening to you vent about classes until we both began giggling over—as you termed it—"tales of doom and woe from Zoom school."

This is a small example of how solutions emerge when we *yield* to obstacles. We understand "problems" that "shouldn't be there" as nothing less than the human journey itself. We accept what is, and *love* reality—regardless of the form it takes.

Such wisdom also applies to far worse situations than family squabbles. Consider, for instance, how Rubin "Hurricane" Carter practiced amor fati. A top contender for the US middleweight title in the mid-1960s, this African American man was wrongly accused of triple homicide. He went on trial, and a biased, bogus verdict resulted in three life sentences. Remarkably, Hurricane refused to view himself as powerless, even as he invested extensive time in his often frustrating legal case. Though trapped bodily, Hurricane never relinquished the knowledge of himself as a free human as he refused to wear a uniform, accept visitors, attend parole hearings, or even work in the commissary to reduce his sentence. The guards responded by throwing him in solitary confinement for weeks on end, but Carter would come out whistling.

It took nineteen years and two trials to overturn that verdict, but when Carter walked out of his cell, he simply resumed life. He didn't launch a civil suit to recover damages, nor did he request an apology from the court. Such actions would have implied something was taken from him when—to Carter—nothing ever was. Even within a "Reef" that ensnared him, he chose to practice *amor fati*. Since his mind was free, he was better able to act in positive ways that would ultimately free his body too.

This afternoon, just as it started to drizzle, I noticed someone beside the river below Mill House Bridge: Baltimore poet Michael Hugues, with a pen pressed against a notebook page, stalking stanza in ripples. Michael is thirty, with a shaved head and light beard. Each day he dons similar black clothes—reminding me of your new favorite color—and he always sits at the same corner table in the Mill House dining room, beside an open window.

"Listen!" he whispered the other day when I sat beside him. Beneath the din of conversations and silverware on plates, I heard the Gihon River cascade below. Michael hails from blue-collar roots, and from what I've gleaned about his life, it has not been an easy one. He lives frugally, earning his money woodworking, something he also loves, and writes his poems slowly, one per day, and hand-binds small books which he fills with his poetry. He travels around Maryland selling the books at cost at festivals. One of the other artists described him to me as "in the 'praise poet' tradition."

Michael saw me and gestured me over to the riverbank now, excitedly. "'There's only one question: *How to love the world*,'" he said, reciting poet Mary Oliver. "Let me keep company with those who say 'Look!' and laugh with astonishment and bow their heads.'"

The late Oliver, a praise poet like Michael, had a traumatic early life. Sexually abused by her father, she ran away from home at about your age, and struggled for years to discover *amor fati*-style praise. Michael kept silent for a moment, and then continued to recite Oliver, more softly: "'What I want in my life is *to be willing to be dazzled*, to cast aside the weight of facts.'"

A plump drop fell on the tip of my nose, and my mind spit out a fact: it takes an average of thirty-thousand years for a raindrop like this one to become a raindrop again, after, for instance, seeping through soil, becoming stream, then ocean, until finally transpiring into a rain cloud. I laughed at myself.

A poet reminds me to cast aside complexity for a moment and be dazzled—by a drop.

Just as the "treetop" visualization reorients me within a larger and interconnected pattern, I am helped when I reflect on how those who came before me—"Hurricane" Carter, Mary Oliver, my own ancestors—dealt with challenges. Could it not also help us, *hija*, to reflect on how both we ourselves and our own ancestors might come to love what is?

Faced with threats like escalating climate chaos and deep technological disruption of an ecology which includes humans, is it realistic—or is it utopian—to practice *amor fati*?

How might your ancestors have faced painful situations? What about "Gaia" or another of your own descendants? Might they accept, *or even love,* scenarios as difficult or worse than Hurricane Carter's?

What sources of readily available beauty and softness might you imagine for them? For yourself?

Sixteen

Citadel

Gaia's Seed

Chapter Two

September 23rd, 2131 (Two years later)

Dear *Bisabuela*,

"No more raspberries, Mama," Julia told me yesterday as we walked the hedge path toward our wooden gate to town. For a few weeks she and I had been stopping to feed ourselves each morning. Amid those bushes, we'd sit in bramble shade and pop raspberries into each other's mouths. A fortnight back, the bushes stopped giving, but Julia continued to pause to touch the branches. The dozenth time, Julia stopped, pointed up, and said, "No more raspberries." I realized she now knows not only that her food comes from the earth, but also that her food, sometimes, *does not come from the earth*. Seasons.

Back in the Domain, I understood nothing of this. I Realitied whatever I wanted, and I wanted far, far more than year-round raspberries. Not limited by the five senses humans inhabit, as a bracomi I could intuit, for example, a thought like "beach" and instantly be in Bali. Or I'd think "monk" and enter the stillest, solemnest Tibetan seclusion. From the bracomi perspective, what "Primitives" like you—and like *me*, today—call reality is mere lusterless 3D. I used to Reality vast intelligence through dozens of engineered senses that are nothing like crude early 21st-century "virtual reality." Bracomis have integrated *organic* microchips and what you used to call "smart fluids" into a seamless and potent sense of pleasure . . . and power.

In Johnson, we have no off-season produce. Julia and the rest of us eat only from what Pachamama gives, but, in merging with the Earth's massive generative rhythms, we access another sort of pleasure—and power. In the evenings, especially, and sometimes during my four-in-the-morning restlessness over our coming exile, I think of how connected little Julia is to the cycles of light as she plays with Luna and Boots under the single light on our porch at night. Julia will come inside, half-crying, complaining that Luna's been too rough. Jim goes out and gently disciplines Luna, then returns, leaving our daughter outside to further bond with her animals in the night.

There's another nocturnal routine that Calder and I have oft enacted. I'll be in the hammock and Calder, across the porch, switches off the light. Darkness. Silence. We listen.

Crooak, calls a frog, eventually, from the little pond behind our peach trees.

"Frogs!" Calder then exclaims in a loud whisper, running full speed over to the hammock to clamber onto my body, wiggling her chest into mine for protection. Then we listen together.

The frog's patterned call tends to stop, and when it does, he breaks our embrace. "The frogs are asleep," he says, matter-of-factly. Then Calder climbs down, switches on the light again, and turns it off. We repeat the same routine.

I don't remember exactly when he invented this game, but it grew naturally out of his existence as a mammal on the land: bring on darkness; listen for perilous wilderness calls; run to Mama Bear's arms.

Guess these will belong to my "land memories." Ah, *Bis*, so much has happened since I last wrote you. The Domain has enacted something far worse. Our worst nightmare: a program of Elimination.

Now none of the tens of thousands of North American human settlements are safe. A network of human spies, 'bots, and a smattering of sympathetic bracomis usually forewarn us of Domain raids, but "usually" isn't holding it in Johnson anymore. Last polis, two-thirds of us voted for preemptive evacuation . . . to the ocean.

The seas are our next frontier. We don't have another apparent choice, so I embrace it as an adventure. Our plan is to caravan all of Johnson, in small groups so we're more covert, to a New Hampshire bay where a 350-person-capacity ship awaits. Last week I packed family grab bags since our evacuation window could be just five hours. Meanwhile, Jim's away evacuating Morrisville to a cove in southern Maine. I've been closing down the farm without seeming to close it down: wilding the sheep, camouflaging the hydrogant (again), freeze-drying just about everything. Whew. Jim has already arranged and stealthed our ship in North Carolina, and its way up the coast to us now. My husband's not been sleeping more than two hours a night, which he can do more easily now that my he's ... bridged.

So: a maximum 3 percent of us now "bridge" human and bracomi via fluids and chips. As provisional cyborgs, our Bridgers have the artificial brainpower to invent essential survival tech, such as interhuman communications encryption and ocean stealth. We humans are fierce localizers, so it was only grudgingly and out of necessity that we patched together a federation of our communities. The federation decided late last year that, in order to survive, some of us must re-volve–but only selectively, so as to preserve our humanity.

You see, we're easy prey on land because bracomis control the continents. That's their base for vital infrastructure, and they've tolerated our communities until now because we weren't really a threat. But with the surge in defections in our direction and growing eco-tage actions against bracomi infrastructure, the Domain is stiffening into despotism. Forty-plus human towns have already been atomized, and thousands of our leaders, Bridgers among them, have been jailed, their brain-data vamped.

But we can go stealth onto the oceans because, after the Cusp, when the world's population fell to 1.2 billion, land became plentiful. There were far fewer bipeds around to exploit it. On top of that, most of the 1.2 billion were bracomis and, therefore, engineered to have carbon footprints as innocuous as an average Bangladeshi back in your time. Irony of ironies?

But bracomis got so hooked on Mars jaunts and money-spinning asteroid mining that they mostly ignored the oceans, and that was our opening. We've been rounding up abandoned boats: moored and dry-docked cruise ships, fishing trawlers, yachts, freight tankers, and even aircraft hangars. Jim and other Bridgers recommission them as floating eco-villages stealthed in codes bracomi still can't break.

The bottleneck is getting to our ships over a perilous land crossing. One in five evacuating humans is killed en route. Jim is working with eastern-Oregon Bridgers to better our terrestrial stealth, and the Underground Railroad is a boon, but I worry for your great-*great*-grand kids, *Bisabuela*.

Since I'm ready to evac the kids and me on the spot, there's time for quietude, so I write to you, and I split logs we'll never get to burn. Out of the silence this afternoon while I was stacking firewood, I heard an accusation pop out of nowhere, clear as a Hollywood Age voice-over: "*Luddite!*" I whirled around. Nobody there, of course, and I laughed. I guess, like most Johnsonites, I'm a Primitive and proud of it.

It makes me recall something our just-evacuated, Austrian-descent neighbors, the Berghahns, used to do. They'd make their kids "earmuff" whenever they passed a house or vehicle playing bracomi music. I once asked the dad about it as we stood in front of Maverick Studios, an apartment building where they lived in one of several flats we created after the Domain abandoned the VSC sim. He said: "It's self-explanatory if you think about it."

Then there's our friend Mateo. He reads nothing written after the year 1900. And I think of our own acres, similarly buffered from Domain "modernity." While I happily use blenders, hydrogants, and the alternet, I'm a sensualist in love with the feel of wind on skin and creek on feet, with the sight of a vulture soaring, right now, skimming our orchard canopy, nearsighted in its carrion quest. (Hey, after all I'm Gaia, *verdad*?) I often feel like Emily Dickinson: an "inebriate of Air . . . a Debauchee of Dew." If I look sideways at my family's plunge into the human enigma, I see children and dogs running down our dirt road. I hear friends' laughter and *Me want food* and family *Cooou-ie* calls. Yet these are already ripples.

"Enjoying some alone time?" our neighbor, Jaime, asked me this morning, no shortage of sarcasm in his tone. Longtime Vermonters from the southern part of the state, the earlobe-plugged, long-bearded Jaime, and his wife, Balu, work as silversmiths. Their two Julia-aged daughters, a pair of horses, and a throng of chickens are the backwoods backdrop against which the couple have always forged jewelry in the pergola visible to me now beyond our beech-windbreak.

"Here to say *adios y nos vemos* starboard," Jaime said, taking my hand in a firm grip. Over his shoulder, I spotted Balu loading their rickshaw with backpacks, her dreadlocks falling over a homemade dress drawn taut by a pregnant belly. Jaime noticed my open notebook and flashed me a questioning look. I told him I was writing to you. Hadn't told anyone but Jim about this odd habit of mine.

Jaime flicked a fly from his beard, pondering this as he gazed down toward the Gihon-side yurt of Evan and Lucio, a bracomi-devolved gay couple. Calder was climbing the massive yurt-side oak with two of the couple's three adopted kids while the smallest, Regalito, played in the sandbox with Julia. Evan and Lucio tend the general store on Main and also homestead, like we all do.

Even as we're about to decamp Johnson, I'm newly astounded that *eleven* houses rise around us. Jim and I were the first to settle this slope eight years ago. When we arrived, all we could see were birch, meadows, and whippoorwills. I feel devastated about the badgers and beavers, the moose and elk that used to live on our land and the larger acreage of subdivided territory with all these new homes. We pushed those native species up into the steeper, still-wild forests of the Green Mountains above.

Jaime and Balu, Evan and Lucio, Jim and me–all with kids under five, have staked out boundary lands on the edge of Johnson, constructed our earth homes, laid water pipes. *Species radiation,* biologists call it, the way animals spread through a given habitat, taking possession of new territory until they are stopped by a counterforce. It's because we humans radiated so successfully that the bracomi now want to be that counterforce. A part of me understands their position since our homesteading resembles that of our 19th-century-"pioneer" ancestors and their Manifest Destiny creed. While the bracomis, ironically, burn zero carbon, we humans sprawl into forests and gulp energy. *Have* we, after all, changed deeply enough?

Lost in this reverie, Jaime's irritated voice startled me. Seemingly out of nowhere, he said: "Tell her she screwed up!"

"I'm *sorry*?" I said.

"*A la mierda* with our new moon meditations and nonviolent sociocracy for a minute. Write and ask your *Bisabuela* why her cohort sat on their butts in the 2050s while billionaire offspring like iLon Musk and Billy QQX Gates piloted themselves as bracomi beta, their New Borg charisma hooking everyone on Final Evolve."

Jaime, breathing hard now, let this settle. Balu, hearing her husband's tone, interrupted her packing and walked toward us as he continued: "Ask your *Bis*," Jaime continued, "what the heck *was not* blatantly apparent to her generation, even back in the 2020s, when Musk and Gates, Sr., publicly lauded brain-chipping and in-vitro cloned-meat skyscrapers. Corporations in her day didn't even hide their plans. Ask Grandma why her generation chose to look away! Worse, they *joined* in!"

Balu approached and placed a hand on Jaime's shoulder. I knew their family was stressed about leaving. Jim and I had overheard their near-daily arguments. She whispered to Jaime that they needed to finish loading the rickshaw.

Then she looked at me with her large oval eyes, sad now. Her pod was leaving tonight, for the port outside Citadel where we'd meet them again. Hopefully. She took Jaime's hand and gazed at her feet. She seemed to silently say: "I ache every day for the kids. How will they survive floating on salt water for years?"

Then she looked up at me. When our eyes linked, hers got teary. "No *trees*, Gaia," she said, crying. "No more Gihon."

October 5th, 2131

Dear *Bisabuela*,

As our milk truck dropped into Citadel today, a surreal scene unspooled.

I watched the eccentric scene fly by: cupolas, cowboy-hatted farmers and hoop-skirted Iroquois, persimmon trees, a geodesic dome, a black Brahmin cow wandering down the side of the road, flicking its tail, and productive little orchards wrapping around and through everything. We wound up a narrow track to our destination: Citadel Acres announced a colorful, hand-painted sign above the words *Organic Farm, B&B, Herbalario, and Garden Café.*

The four of us stepped out into the unfamiliar scent of the sea. A terraced acre of a hundred varieties of edible plants and a "Spices and Essential Oils Workshop" over-looked a narrow estuary feeding the Atlantic Ocean a couple of miles away. I squinted toward the port, spying it down there amid hundreds of human dwellings along the rocky coast. I hardly had time to take this all in when Citadel Acres co-owner Thorsten Haque was suddenly bounding down a footpath toward us.

The uber-tall, seventy-something proprietor had to duck under a bluebell arbor to reach us. A wool jockey's cap over his bouncy gray curls, he gave Calder a hug crushing enough to make my son gasp. Behind Thorsten, gliding with a serene, Buddhist-monk gait, came his short-haired, also seventy-ish wife, Isabel. They'd both "worked" as psychologists in the Domain but treasoned two decades back. While traveling through the area in 2108, they went AWOL after falling in love with Citadel's slow life. They purchased thirteen acres of degraded cat-tle pasture and cultivated the parched hillside. Thorsten led our welcome tour, enthusing that "each part of Citadel Acres blossomed instinctively, *without* an overall design." The place did feel like less of a business than an ecologically-centered community of employees, neigh-bors, and short- and long-term volunteers and guests, human and bracomi alike.

The illusion is flawless. This crossed my mind as Isabel and Thorsten shepherded us to the three-bedroom, hob-bit-like, strawbale house where we'd stay while awaiting our ship's arrival—fingers tightly crossed—in a few days. We stepped into the hush of rounded earth walls, a wood-burning stove, an arched ceiling held by a vaulting single-birch post, and a stunning mural, a rendition of a Phoenix coming out of the ashes. Calder gazed up, awed, at the high ceiling inlaid with fine bamboo. Handcrafted wooden beds were prepped with crisp linens, and we had a view. over cultivated fields, of the glistening estuary.

Our Underground Railroad hosts smiled, noticing how much we appreciated all they'd prepared for us. Isabel handed us cups of "heirloom apple juice" and said–and what hit me in the gut was Isabel's intonation, identical to human speech–"*Dejanos saber* if there's anything else you need."

I strain to hear the ocean tonight as I write to you on an unfamiliar bed, in this safehouse. *We're so close*, I think to myself with a lump in my throat.

Jim and the kids are still in a full-blown pillow fight in the living room. Twenty minutes ago I stole away to write, exhausted from whacking *mis hijitos* with padded missiles. I'd tallied up fourteen direct pillow-hits to Calder's zero, and he laughed more blissfully than I'd heard since leaving home. Now I hear Jim proclaiming yet again, *Pillow fight's over* and *Bedtime!* But the pair of them continues to wrestle their dad down and yell "sneak attack!" At last, Jim announces a conclusive end: "Too much pillow fighting!"

Calder replies, earnestly: "Daddy, you can *never* have too much pillow fighting."

Emotions. They swirl through me. Isabel and Thorsten's impeccable speech brought on memories of the day I began to reclaim my own voice. On the morning I crossed the river to Jim.

How to explain? Bracomis, *Bis*, don't have language the way you know it. Similar to using your era's phones to connect the thoughts of two people thousands of miles away through voice, bracomis use "inner phones" and communicate neither through external gadgets nor as uttering animals. Their cerebral chips transmit at a thousand times the velocity of your smart phones through a kind of inner Wi-Fi. For example, as a bracomi I could communicate the contents of all of Gabriel García Márquez novels to another 'borg in Asia Domain in four seconds. Ideas short of Gabo's opus transmit instantly. Over the decades, the bracomi tongue, jaw, and larynx atrophied, like the human appendix withering through disuse. In the Domain of my day, we bracomi could only grunt, but who even bothered?

But now they've Enhanced into speech. I've had so little contact with bracomis that I didn't know the tech existed. When I asked our hostess Isabel about it, she averted her eyes. "Just a fluid adjustment, *nada mas*," she mumbled, quickly shifting the subject to linens and "farm-crafted soap." I think she's self-conscious about slumming it human.

It's an open secret that she and Thorsten never de-volved, and that attend virtual saturnalian orgies every Wednesday night. Some of us disparage such 'borgs as *cuellas de goma*, rubber necks, because they do one-eighty turns at will, but I have nothing against them. It doesn't matter that Thorsten and Isabel didn't cut the cord like I chose to. Bracomi mavericks—not just high-profile infiltrators and moles, but also everyday safe-housers like our hosts—contribute to how our spe-cies has radiated so deeply into fresh territory. Without decent Underground Railroad bracomi like Isabel and Thorsten, how would we even *get* to our ships?

While we're on the subject of tolerance, I need to say that I don't blame your generation for apathy or inaction, Great-grandma, the way my former neighbor Jaime does.

What Jaime forgets is that plenty in your day knew how to create localized community and also how to

manage inner thoughts and emotions as organic humans . . . *without* converting into bracomis. Millions of
you were forming urban Transition streets and eco-villages and innovating exactly as we did in Johnson or
like they're doing in Citadel. But millions, in the huge
context of billions of people, wasn't enough. It would be
easy for me to wag a finger at you and complain that if
enough people in your era had possessed the courage
to stay human, you could have, collectively, prevented
much hurt in 2131. But if I've learned one thing in this
one Mama's crisis-filled life, it's this: love alone opens
all doors, no matter how tightly closed, including those
between past and future.

Even amid trauma, Jim and I find ways to open our
hearts each day amid the complicated emotional dynamic of his Bridging. In our respective transitions, each
of us has moved closer to where the other one started,
so in many ways we now understand each other better.
We've had some tear-soaked evenings because it's been
like a bad trip for him, sometimes, the barrage of *every-
thing-ness* after you chip-up. He also knows now, as I do,
about how eerily mesmerizing it is to be polymorphously
brilliant. Amazing, yes. *Joyful*, no. Are joy and our natural
senses the same? Maybe, because almost none of our
Bridgers–despite having seen the "superior" side–have
been tempted back! And this is despite Domain's blanket
amnesty policy for Bridgers and humans who voluntarily
defect to the Domain. Only a handful of us have flipped
to bracomi, even as tens of thousands defect our way.

Jim and I do things like remembering, every day, that
this day could be our last. And if it is, that's the right day
to relinquish our bodies. Whenever it ends, it will have
been enough.

The alternative is to fear the bracomis. After all, they
could surprise us at any moment, and then of course we

die. But if we fear them—fear death—we become that fear and therefore miss out on life. Our lifespan is not set at three-hundred, or even eighty. Our lives are *now* ... in our spooning at night, in our pillow fights with the kids.

Now, as Jim corrals Calder and Julia into their pajamas, I remember that morning at the Vermont Studio Center simulation when he returned for me. (Jim would later tell me that, on his first sighting, he found me as racy as I found him!) Staring at him from my VSC Thoreau studio window, out toward the Gihon's far bank, and, afraid he might flee, I took the stairs two at a time to the foyer. I flung Maverick Studios's door open and ran down the ridge to river's edge. Panting, I walked to a point directly across the water from him.

Jim could have shouted over to me since the river at that juncture was just forty feet across. But he stood in silence with a mournful look, and I felt a magnetism, sharp and fresh.

My bladder still worked, it occurred to me then: so what about my Primitive ovaries? Bracomis are enhanced out of fertility so as not to spawn "Primitives" and are instead synthesized from human DNA. Though this is changing as so many bracomis—like Thorsten and Isabel—go rogue, bracomis like me were set for power-down at three hundred, the Domain having determined that lifespan as compatible with a Sustainable World. But that day on the river's edge, I wondered if my body could still reproduce.

The man who would become father to *your* great-great-grandchildren then slipped out of his sandals and stepped into the river. And I wondered what it would be like to leave the security of the Domain. To swim across to him.

That's when it happened. Out of nowhere, a sound surged from my throat. The piercingly gorgeous note of an aria streamed forth. With all our verbal atrophy, I couldn't believe I still had the windpipe for song.

But when the music I thought I'd made echoed back from the foothills, it sickened me. I'd actually barked out a mutant howl. Embarrassed, reflex caused my hand to shoot up to my withered vocal cords.

I thought he would recoil, but his sorrowful expression remained. He took another step into the river. My pulse sped up when he reached out a hand. A human was tempting me across.

Seventeen

The Knife

And the rain in the night, driven
by the loneliness of the wind
to perforate the darkness.

—John O'Donohue

Hijita,

Not long before I met Melissa, you and I were apart for a time. How I missed you, as I struggled in my native New York City to work and send funds back to you and your mother in Bolivia. I felt Separated as I attempted to live disconnected from water. Manhattan and Brooklyn are shored by a beautiful estuary, that brackish juncture of the Hudson and East Rivers with the Atlantic. But when I sat on the pylons of Pier 45 and stuck my bare feet into the Hudson, somebody called the cops on me for trespassing. And in Williamsburg, Brooklyn, I took off my shoes and stepped into the East River, but a security guard removed me.

The only place I could step into water was in the Bronx. Sometimes, between my writing and NYU teaching sessions,

I would take the subway there to spend hours with chimpanzees, elephants, tigers, and macaws. Sick of my species, of
myself. And the only way I could be with other species was
to visit them in cages. It all seemed so ominous. On the way
out of the zoo, I'd walk to one of the only stretches of river-
ine woods in New York, strip to my boxers, and cannonball
into a Hudson tributary's cold floor. It was contaminated,
but I didn't care because there was peace down there. Author
Chellis Glendinning, in her book *My Name Is Chellis and I'm
in Recovery from Western Civilization,* talks about how mental
illness is often related to our great modern split from nature, a
split that was clearly splitting me. At the bottom of the Bronx
River, I felt myself stitch up, if only a bit, finding what resem-
bled the one square inch of silence in the city.

To try and cheer myself, I would recall a beloved Japanese
Zen teacher, the late Dogen-Zenji who, whenever he drew
water from his monastery's river outside Kyoto, would return
half of each dipper to the river. When humans really see the
beauty of a river, this is what they do. The bridge leading to
Dogen's monastery is called 橋 柄杓, or Half-Dipper Bridge,
to remind today's visitors about a reciprocity with nature
we've mostly lost.

To remain "up" I'd also remember how, as a child, my parents gave me Territory. There, I began to discover and steward
a space I'd come to know as my inner acre.

When I was six, my parents moved us out of our box-turtle-
bulldozed Ronkonkoma neighborhood to a house farther
out on Long Island. There I would live until I was eighteen,
sleeping each night in a treehouse of sorts, since the roof of
my second-story bedroom slanted down into tree branches
which would brush night rain against the windows, acorns
drumming the roof a foot above my head. Our yard was a
maze of half-wild footpaths through thick oak and pine forest,
some of the paths looping back into themselves. Between our
home and the three-block walk down a backroad to my school

was an island of woods surrounded by suburban development. We loved the croaking of frogs, the trill of terns, the splash of guppies in the enormous *swamp* in the center of those woods. Trees shimmered and spoke above, the edgy human aspect somehow part of this weird, wild otherness of voice.

We kids spent much time in that sizable tract of buffer forest between our street on the one side and the school property on the other, our mammal bodies drawn into this expanse. We sank bare feet into the mud of the swamp and balanced on the large, exposed roots of fallen trees; birds and raccoon and possum and humans, soft animal bodies loving what they love. We were drawn there as kids because, from the DNA in our big toes to the synapses in the brain, we are all hardwired to dwell in such habitats.

From these childhood acres I later discovered that I had something parallel inside me. Something fertile, golden, and aglow with life: an inner acre.

What I learned was that your inner acre, once you've discovered and inhabited it, becomes the impenetrable facet of your interior power. If action is what you do when you still have some control over a situation, your inner acre is there to depend on when agency has all but disappeared. A situation that seems unchangeable and indisputably adverse can be turned into a learning experience, a humbling experience, a chance to comfort others. But your inner acre needs to be first encountered, and then cultivated. Humble, resilient, and flexible, it is a space of sustainable retreat. The opposite of withdrawal to your inner acre is the rush to act in spite of terrible odds, but this is usually weakness disguised by fast-life bristle.

In New York, during the time we were apart, I lost contact with my inner acre. In those *Don't step in the water* days, I would purchase ten-dollar phone cards at the Indian-owned shop near my row house on Elliot Avenue in Queens. I'd punch in the Telecard's code and then your Bolivian number. "*Hola,*

Papá!" you'd squeal when you heard my voice. At that point in your life, we still spoke only Spanish together, and you'd tell me in your delightful eastern-Bolivian *camba* accent about your kittens and puppy and the mango tree in your urban allotment. And after *te quiero mucho*'s, we'd hang up, and I'd be away, without you, with a few dollars left on a Telecard in Queens.

Partly in an effort to feel closer to Territory, to you, I sought out Latin dives, thinking to find some essence of Bolivia in Jackson Heights. Far from the trendy Manhattan joints like Copacabana, were satellites of Santa Cruz, Bolivia, in sweaty Queens joints like Hairos. There, a two-dollar cover included a raffle ticket. The beer was cheap, and everyone danced in the confined space, people not just from Bolivia, but from all over South America and the Caribbean, from *América Centrál y México*.

On a particular Saturday night, as the music pulsed, I tried to feel good, but a beat-down and estranged quality pounded beneath the rhythms. There were many others in Hairos, after all, who also walked down to a corner shop to purchase a Telecard. I'd seen plenty of folks like the ones dancing around me buying Telecards. In fact, those of us with kin across the border were the only ones buying them. Most of the folks who purchased discount Telecards and two-dollar Jackson Heights covers were purchasing what they could afford, after an off-the-books week vacuuming the apartments and polishing the dishes of Separation. Vulnerability pounded beneath the salsa. Unease filled me, and I knew that this place was not closer to you, to Territory. I left Hairos before the midnight raffle and boarded an elevated subway, and everything felt just so hard. Hard as New York's asphalt, hard as the polluting Hummers below the train.

I once owned a knife with an ironwood handle and a blade that gleamed like water. I share something of my shadow, *hija*, not to discourage you, but rather to convey the pain, as well as the boon, of anybody's journey to their inner acre.

The same night of the HP dolphin-chipping panel, I went to the IFC—a favorite haunt for independent films in the heart of the West Village—to see the documentary *When a Tree Falls*, about a group of eight Oregon college students and assorted young Earth-protectors who were examining their own relationship to Separation. After these young women and men marched in rallies and occupied trees in platforms to halt the destruction of the final 4 percent of the United States' old growth forest, they determined societally acceptable efforts to be futile; so they joined together through the Earth Liberation Front (ELF), a decentralized collective of activists, and began to monkey wrench.

The film focuses on the erstwhile twenty-four-year-old Daniel McGowan, a fresh-faced young environmental activist who went to high school in Middle Village, Queens, the same neighborhood where your own working-class great-grandparents raised your grandfather (my dad). McGowan, having by then moved to Oregon, spent weeks with his friends scouting out the remote Superior Lumber Company's equipment warehouse, which contained the machinery capable of destroying a forest. When these new ELF members—known as "elves"—were completely certain that no person was within miles of the remote wilderness warehouse, the group set a controlled burn that did not touch the forest but, rather, destroyed one-million-dollars' worth of bulldozers, chainsaws, and other equipment. In this way the freshly minted outlaws felt they'd temporarily protected thousands of acres of pristine old-growth forest and the wild animals living in that habitat. Then the eco-saboteurs vanished.

The care they took to ensure no human life was taken was consistent with fifty years of US monkey wrenching, or "ecotage" (ecological sabotage), during which time not a single nonactivist has been injured, and nobody has died. Principle number one of ELF, ALF (the Animal Liberation Front), and kindred groups is: life above all else. And while I do not normally condone arson, shouldn't there be proportionality between an action and its consequences? Oregon judges did not think so. They ruled that property *is* life, and that those students were therefore murderers. Around the same time, the FBI declared ecotage to be "the biggest source of domestic terrorism," and the media gave our rebellious elves a new label: "ecoterrorists."

The case of the Oregon group went cold. The ELF network was airtight, keeping their oaths of secrecy. Many of the saboteurs left direct action ecotage for slower, above-board work in environmental-justice nonprofit organizations. But the FBI continued to hunt them, spending millions of dollars over years in Operation Backfire. An arson case of similar insurance value, even if it were a corporate warehouse, would have long since been filed "unsolved," but not when the Story of Separation has been challenged.

Years later, they did find a weak link. They gave the "elf" whom they arrested a Sophie's choice: either life in prison with no possibility of parole or freedom *if* he used a concealed microphone to record his friends' confessions. The FBI flew him around the country to pretend to bump into fellow elves, thereby obtaining several confessions. Then, during a simultaneous nationwide sting, Daniel McGowan's nonprofit office in New York was raided, and he and others from the Oregon warehouse ecotage were arrested. The FBI offered the tree huggers seven-year prison sentences if they gave evidence against their cohorts . . . or else they'd get life sentences.

After the film I left the IFC theater and emerged, a little dazed, out onto the Sixth Avenue sidewalk.

There, the young Mrs. McGowan, Daniel's wife, stood behind a table of brochures and a petition. She told me her husband is in a maximum-security prison in the Midwest, locked up with serial killers. She has not seen him for years. He gets one half-hour phone call per month. As I signed her petition to improve McGowan's prison conditions, I sensed the low burn of rage and, with it, the gravity of a knife. Going home, the subway grinding from stop to stop, I felt guilty at being secure and comfortable when Daniel McGowan and a thousand others chafed in prisons for defending Gaia—our Earth—against Reef-madness. *No compromise in defense of Mother Earth*, exclaim Earth First! and ELF activists as they monkey wrench, and maybe they're right. I pictured the SUVs in my own neighborhood spewing carbon and sending other species into extinction. I imagined what I could do with the knife in my drawer.

If I couldn't take down the Reef, at least I could inflict damage upon it. I pictured the hundreds of Land Cruisers and Hummers in my area of Queens. Americans already consume, per capita, the resource equivalent of four planet Earths. Even in a city with a good subway system, these drivers flaunted six-mpg guzzlers. How satisfying would it feel to slash dozens of SUV tires, leaving a symbolic MTA subway card under the wipers of each stranded vehicle?

It's no major act of monkey wrenching, but for a respectable professor like me, it seemed enormous as a gateway deed into political radicalism. My thinking was more rigid at the time, my passion inflamed by facts and perceived injustices. I felt isolated and separated from nature, from water. I had not yet embarked with Melissa upon a joyful path of helping to create intentional living.

That cloudy night I heard distant thunder as I walked into the streets with my sheathed knife. Although nobody was out, aside from the occasional passerby on the main boulevard, steel enemies were plentiful. They formed regimented lines along the curbs, block after block, walling each street like lifeless corals.

I identified the first target, a black Hummer shadowed from the streetlights by a horse chestnut tree. I unsheathed the knife and imagined that after this first tire, I could do dozens more and, having thus sabotaged, move on to bigger actions. My Separated ego built this up as cutting my teeth as a purveyor of ecotage.

I jammed the blade into the rear tire of the Hummer. Fully inflated, the tire rebuffed my knife.

I changed positions to lean into the handle with my shoulder and caught sight of something reflected in the blade: my own face, barely visible in the darkness, and the blurred shapes of horse chestnut trees blowing in the background as rainclouds moved over. In the blade I saw a face no different from those of the Hummer owners, and I knew that disabling this vehicle would not wound a system. Should I puncture this tire and a hundred more, should I burn a thousand chainsaws, all would be replaced.

I turned the blade to my wrist. I knew I had the power to end at least one part of Separation. I'd seen Gaia's enemy, and it was me. The Stoics I admired held up suicide as the last-resort "back door" out of a situation when society has completely closed off the possibility of the philosopher to live justly. They saw the natural human mind and heart as most sacred, so it was ethical to choose death over capitulation of one's inner sanctity to a larger evil. This is what Stilesto felt when he lay down, pierced his own heart with a knife, and let it bleed out. Socrates, with a cup of hemlock. Seneca, too, took his own life instead of relenting to the tyrant Nero.

I don't know what I would have done if she hadn't come.

Unexpectedly, I felt her touch on my neck. Then I caught

her fresh fertile scent, and the knife's blade freckled with droplets. It was *her*: the night rain.

I tasted a drop of water and remembered the Territories your grandparents gave me: the box-turtle woods. The feel of my bare feet in swamp mud. My inner acre. Pressing the blade tip into my finger, I saw blood pool and felt mammal pain. Walking home, I touched the sides of my head—these temples, for now, still human—and that's when I remembered your name.

When you were an infant, *hija*, under the mango tree in the simple outdoor courtyard of your Santa Cruz home, I dipped you in water and gave you your name.

During your *bautismo de agua*, or water baptism, I passed you to your maternal grandmother, who passed you to your Bolivian grandpa. Then you were gently shared with *tío* Eduardo, *tía* Alison, and *tía* Alejandra. Each person kissed your forehead. We ate quail eggs and drank Champagne, pouring the first few drops onto the ground to give thanks to Pachamama.

You cried out when I dipped your infant head in water. Then I touched your soft temples and spoke into your ear a name which means "beloved first daughter" in Quechua—and this you are. It also means "spirit" in Aymara, which is to say, you are made of mystery.

Amaya, I whispered.

There is a final meaning to your name, and it is of underground significance. It's a foundational name interconnecting you with your Amazon and Celtic animist ancestors who were slain for putting life above Progress. It relates you to those persecuted today for loving the life force, from Sea Shepherds to the imprisoned elves from my own New York neighborhood. It connects you to the future, where humans who remember their names may come under harsh chafing.

We baptized you human with a maverick name that bubbled forth from Dogen-Zenji. Beneath Half-Dipper Bridge, the peaceful monk proffered water back to the river, and in the evenings he listened to the humble rhythm of 雨夜, or *Amaya*, falling down and down. Your name in Japanese is Night Rain.

Drops fall in Vermont's darkness, whispering *remember*. They fall, as they fell on me that dark-but-sacred night of discovery when I held a knife and blood flowed. I say your name to the Gihon tonight as I drop a paper leaf. *Night Rain*. Falling unseen, it streams toward you.

V

Ocean

Eighteen

Freedom from Ambition

I can't wait to get back home to you.

I imagine dancing with you at your *quinceañera*. How fun it was yesterday, on a three-way video call with Melissa, to plan your celebration, which will take place at our house: a dinner catered by our chef friend from Cochabamba, six or seven of your closest Samaipata *amigos* gathered, and a sleepover in the living room to follow. Traditionally, a father performs a *quinceañera* waltz with his daughter as she passes into adulthood, but I'm sure we'll improvise some of the upbeat salsa we've long danced together.

The other part of our conversation surprised me: you've distanced yourself from longtime friends and are questioning your education. After a decade in the same school, you think you'd like to switch.

I knew that you and your friends had been drifting apart over the past year, but I didn't realize that *"siempre habia divisiones dentro de 'las cumpas'"*—There's always been divisions in *las cumpas*. The crux of it: many of your former besties are caught up in what you call a *"cambasico"* mentality, a con-traction of *"camba,"* or Santa Cruz resident, and *"basica,"* or cookie-cutter trend follower. ("Cambasicos," you told us, "listen to reggaeton and other commercial music and wear the exact same clothes.") You're seeking something else.

In the video call, I noticed other changes. You'd painted your nails black and wore a new piece of jewelry you'd made: a recycled can-tab choker. You showed us a photo of the black overbust corset you'd like to get, played us the riot grrrl punk you now like. Your style has been evolving slowly, but now it's snapped into place.

I understand why you'd be feeling torn about your school decision. You appreciate the English-speaking private school you've long attended but now see through the way it's Separated. I've stretched our resources to send you there, and you've said that, while you appreciate the opportunity, you might be done with "prep." You told Melissa and me that the school you'd prefer to attend next year is "more Bolivian": Spanish-speaking, a little gritty, and populated with the fellow riot grrrls who are your new friends.

You told us the clock is ticking—we have exactly a week to decide if you switch schools.

After we hung up I went to the VSC meditation house. Sat on the cushion. Allowed the thoughts to bubble up: *black fingernails. Riot grrrls. Wants to leave her school.* I felt myself questioning your change in style and focus. But inwardly, I popped each bubble.

A half hour passed, and I felt myself floating on another sensation. My thoughts lessened. I began to feel an inner expansion, a series of rings that kept expanding out like countless golden O's. That sense of infinity remained after I left the meditation house. It struck me how limited it would be to judge you for a style that I might not choose but that obviously resonates with you. However, I still felt torn about the wisdom of your changing schools. Was my ambivalence a residue of my bumper sticker conditioning during my time in high school that I wanted, in effect, to protect you by keeping you as "privileged" as possible? Separation's insidious illusions seep into all of us, illusions—and perhaps some realities too—about what will keep us "safe." Whatever the case, I gained more perspective by observing my own monkey mind in meditation.

Later in the day, after our call, I walked to Johnson's cemetery, the question of your switching schools still with me. Hidden in a corner of town, tucked behind some track houses, Lemuel Hill Cemetery, with its thousands of tombstones, was a place I had to actively seek out.

Alone in the sprawling hidden graveyard, I walked the rows of the lower field, where the stones dated to the 1860s and 1870s, and realized that the people underfoot were the contemporaries of Walt Whitman and George Eliot, Thoreau and Henry James. In literature, Melissa and I have together strolled Emerson and Hawthorne's Concord and sauntered the Hudson's banks with Whitman, but those eminent figures are now exactly as dead as the disremembered ones composted into Lemuel Hill.

The headstones themselves didn't go back any further, but I ticked back one century deeper and heard Dr. Johnson's witticisms as he rowed up the Thames in a boat with James Boswell—they're both earth now. My hearing weakened only a touch as I slipped into a seventeenth century alive with the tales of Anne Bradstreet and Moliere, both of whose atoms are now elsewhere within the life force. I scanned the centuries in reverse, arriving at those straddling the year zero, into which the wise Greek and Roman Stoics—Zeno and Chrysopsis, Seneca and my beloved Epictetus—have dissipated. Even these, the illustrious exceptions to oblivion, reside only in a few memory traces.

After my cemetery walk, I marveled at my earlier anguish over something so minor as your switching schools. Your self-confidence in leaving the known *cumpas* for other *compañeros*—ones perhaps more maladjusted to empire—suggests how free you are, Amaya. You're in the river, with millions of others in the present, past, and future as, in your own way, you adventure beyond the Reef and swim into a more maverick teen subculture. As you do so, know that I'll continue to listen to you as you express your own truth, as well as your uncertainties and fears. How grateful this dad feels for yet another teaching from you.

One evening, six or seven years ago, Melissa said to me in our Samaipata living room: "Wait, did you hear that?"

We'd just been rehashing one of our habitual ambition patterns: although content in our community and on our land, we found ourselves questioning for the umpteenth time whether the choice of a simpler life meant we were stepping down from "a larger responsibility to the world." Shouldn't we, we wondered aloud, stay up late struggling to raise more funds for environmental and women's causes? Shouldn't we use our joint contacts to establish a new institute or support a burgeoning local initiative by connecting it to international partners?

This kind of deliberation makes sense when we're *in our heads*, which is to say: in the head Separation wires up for us. But here's the thing about "the ocean": When you *die before you die*, a trillion square inches of aquatic silence *move*, very patiently, grinding such rigid "shoulds" into soft sand.

This is not to say Melissa and I no longer employ our brains. Of course we do. They are a beautiful part of our organic endowment. But within a vast identity of natural existence, even concepts that may sound, or even are, benign—for example, *nonprofit sustainability projects*—begin to be known as *imagined-order fictions*. That's not to say that such projects aren't beneficial. They can be, if doing them begins from deep seeing and being. But in this watercourse journey, the never-stop-improving loop that has long inhabited Melissa's head and mine has lost a bit of power each time we've verbalized it. What used to be an up-close monster shouting, "Feel ashamed of your privilege! Do *more every day* to save the world!" has become a distant whisper that no longer tyrannizes us.

So, when Melissa asked me that question—*Wait, did you hear that?*—I listened. Silence. Finally, I asked her: "Do I hear *what?*"

"That was the sound," she said, "of the last of our ambition draining out."

It took me a couple of beats to absorb her joke. Then I chuckled, and the release felt wonderful. We had an adobe house, some land close to wilderness, a life of contribution within a Transition town, sufficient work giving into the whole, adequate leisure time, and closeness to you. In short, we were discovering the elusive contours of *enough*.

This evening I brought Jasmin her dinner. Since I couldn't fit the dining room tray through the gap in the Reef, I passed the individual items through. Their colors—the green of a spinach salad, the orange-yellow of dal—felt jarringly real and alive against the Reef's ghostly whiteness. Jasmin nodded in thanks. I sensed she wanted to be silent.

As I glanced at Jasmin eating, it struck me how serene she seemed, even joyful, in limiting circumstances. I slumped to the floor on the other side of the Reef and recalled a poem, "The Physics of Happiness," attributed to Albert Camus:

Time in the open air.
Love for another being.
Freedom from ambition.
Creation.

Just those four. What could be *freer from ambition* than making a Reef that will never grace a gallery because it has become the artist's studio itself? It brought to mind Trappist monk Thomas Merton who, after abandoning his worldly possessions to enter Gethsemane Abbey, spoke of "the four walls of my new freedom." Perhaps this was something of what Jasmin was experiencing, walled into her sculpture.

Amaya, I know some of the more rarified ideas and practices here might sound like the sharings of a privileged parent with his privileged offspring. That's because that's what you and I are. Though we live—within a widespread ideology of whiteness—among the more fortunate of the most fortunate species on Earth, we certainly don't have all of the solutions. Or even most of them. In many ways we're the problem.

Yes, I know that globalization causes a lot of people a lot of pain, and perhaps we should wrestle more with the plight of the world's Zarahs. Perhaps we should be talking about *los indigenas de asfalto*—the "pavement Indians" you and I both see hawking trinkets on Cruz's street corners, the Guaraní and Chiquitanos women and men wrested from their Amazonian lands by soy and timber multinationals. Or maybe we should—instead of focusing on decolonizing our own colonized "ambition" tendencies—be asking why the majority of folks, even in the supposedly prosperous Western world, have to grind away daily as little more than human robots at Amazon "fulfillment" centers or telemarket timeshare condos off corporate-composed scripts. Entire books have been written on this alienation process and on structural inequality and escapes from it—from environmentalist Charles Eisenstein's *The More Beautiful World Our Hearts Know is Possible* to economist Juliette Shor's *True Wealth*.

I'm delving into "freedom from ambition" because it's vital that we, the more privileged, decolonize what binds us and thereby strangles the world. It's like Jasmin said to me the other day, from within the Reef: "I don't know if humans are smart enough to survive the next two hundred years on this planet." She paused and added: "But you could put any word in there: are humans *brave* enough? Are humans *kind* enough? Are humans *ready* enough to survive the next two hundred years on this planet?"

Jasmin voiced big challenges, and they may seem unrealistic. But if we really are committed to being a species within Gaia—our earthly home—that supports other species as they support us, then we must act intentionally toward a thriving planet where people are happy and connected. Where we have abundant wildlife, and food we can eat off trees as we walk. Where we stop "improving" and restart *evolving*, naturally and within Gaia's rhythms, taking stock of our real needs: inclusion, participation, meaning, purpose, community, fun, sufficient shelter.

I think the answers are there now, but we need to be honest with ourselves, accepting that people have been trying to change, for a long time, things that are structurally set up to resist shifting. Humans, though, *can* find shift and movement in many ways, and we need to find that flow by listening to our intuition and moving toward a future we want to create together. This starts with something quite difficult: accepting that just because we may be privileged doesn't mean we're right.

Daddy!

I love this letter . . . love the moment with you and Melissa . . . and appreciate that you trust my judgment about new styles and switching schools. Hey, just don't spend tooo much time in the cemetery. :) Oh, and I miss you, too.

I've been thinking a lot about what you wrote about privilege. My experience is a little different from yours. Though I've lived all of my life in Bolivia, and am indigenous through my mom, your ancestors are from Ireland, which can be seen in my freckled white skin and auburn hair. As a kid, I overheard other Bolivians express gratitude to my mom: "Thank you for improving our race," they said. Growing up I have to recognize that my physical features give me privilege, but my heart echoes the story of my Amazon heritage.

During my childhood, my Tacana indigenous grandfather, Papa Mike, drove us around in the only vehicle our extended family owned: the tenacious Volkswagen Beetle you know well. Its engine stopped only with his passing. Fifteen years later, that burgundy car still sits patiently in our Santa Cruz driveway, as if waiting his return.

Once, I asked my grandmother why we didn't fix Papa Mike's Beetle. She explained: "We can't prove it's ours." Like the car's ownership papers, I sometimes feel my identity was in question, perhaps not even fully mine. Stolen by my outward appearance.

I was remembering this morning that, when I was six, my Mojeño uncle honored me with my first bow and arrow, a gesture of respect and protection.

Proudly holding high the indigenous peace flag tied to my arrow, I marched in protests to protect an indigenous territory. During these daring times, I learned to respect indigenous leaders who fight to keep their culture alive, and I traveled with my mom deep into rainforests to communities in harmony with Pachamama. I helped organized workshops about women and civil rights out there. My indigenous side has sparked something strong in me.

This is partly why I'm switching schools. I know you, Mom, and Melissa have worked hard to send me to an English-speaking school, but I'm tired of being surrounded by people who are oblivious to their own country's culture! I'm not *running away though. I'm committed to bridge cultures.*

I welcome where I come from—that beautiful, sometimes lonely space of being mixed race.

Oh, and someday I will get the VW bug back on the road where it belongs. Meanwhile, I embrace my powerful indigenous culture along with my "gringa" side. Being indigenous, it's so clear to me now, improved me. *Not the other way around.*

It's three in the morning, and Johnson town residents and VSC residents alike party together for the last time before the artists and writers scatter. The evening began, as it does each Saturday night, at the weekly karaoke night at Downtown Pizza and Pub on Johnson's Main Street, but this time everybody spilled from there into Mill House basement, then we came out to the riverbank for a night swim. I step away from the group for a moment, thinking of you.

Could any dad, anywhere, feel *any* more pride in how mature you are? It's with love for you in my heart that I rejoin the giddy night energy of my transient tribe. In an era of relentless pressure toward productivity, this kind of festival is maverick since such play burns away something of Separation. Swimming and dunking each other in the Gihon, a small tribe joins a long tradition of *otium*.

As you well know, in traditional Andean culture the beginning of the new year, winter solstice, is a time to burn excess possessions. In the Middle Ages, too, and in the animist ages preceding them, leisurely stretches of communal dancing, resting, and indulging were also times to burn things. In Medieval times, often an *entire month* after harvest was dedicated to leisure, with surplus production bonfired. Grow and generate, yes, but instead of bloating with excess, scorch it. Economies overgenerate, creating surplus. Today, this surplus is reinvested in yet more productivity, which generates yet additional surplus—hence, the Mind-made never stop improving overload yoked to human shoulders.

Of course, in this time of climate change and striving to make all of our actions more sustainable, we're not talking about literally *burning* excess possessions but, rather, metaphorically: as another way of considering what constitutes *enough*. More animist cultures' rites can inspire us to consider, preemptively, how we might "burn" excess by not producing it in the first place, by embedding a different rhythm in our lives that places balance above overproduction.

Hunter-gatherers worked an average of twenty-eight hours a week, and the few of them still around continue to do so. Twenty-eight hours is proven sufficient to provide enough to feed, clothe, and shelter us. The Latin word for leisure is *otium*, and the word for work is *negotium*, or *non*-leisure. Strange, then, the way many of us today clock in fifty-hour weeks of *neg-otium* to try and buy *otium*.

This—and also reading your last letter to me—brings to mind the story of the tablet-toting professional aid official who went into the Bolivian Amazon to convince the indigenous inhabitants to ramp up their productivity through a timber-export start-up. He came across a man strolling in the forest beside a river and eagerly demonstrated the business plan to him, using a PowerPoint deck on his tablet.

After listening, and looking at the slides, the indigenous man asked: "But why should I sweat to do that?"

"So you can save up money," the official replied.

"Why do I need to do that?" he further wondered.

"So you can send your children to college."

"Why do they need college?"

"So they can become professionals and earn good money."

"Why would they need so much money?"

The aid expert, becoming increasingly exasperated with each question, blurted out: "So they can give some of it to you! Then, in the future you can retire and have the chance to stroll carefree through the forest!"

The man replied: "That's what I'm doing right now." And he continued joyfully along on his way.

This parable, and your recent thoughts, convey that Westerners have something significant to learn from indigenous people about *otium* and that in the "upside-down world" beyond the Story of Separation, we must question what we *really* have to share with the world and what we don't. The forest-dweller in the parable didn't see himself as "a subject of Western aid" but rather as a happy person.

That story stops there. But I imagine the aid official having a little epiphany after that encounter.

Maybe he comes to his senses—literally—turning off the tablet and breathing in the fresh rainforest air, noticing a two-toed sloth in the ironwood branches above, reaching up to pick wild pacay and tasting its sweet juice. Perhaps he senses a bit of what the man strolling the forest did. Gratitude. Biophilia. Maybe the expert stows his electronics and hikes after the man, asking to be taught something about the herbal remedies in the forest or about his ancestors' relationship with Pachamama. Maybe he even thinks to himself later that evening: *If we "advanced" Western people can't be happy on this planet at this time—with such abundance—when can we be? Is there a different kind of abundance we might remember?*

Do you remember how I once lived alone for a season in an off-grid, twelve-foot-by-twelve-foot tiny house in North Carolina? It was owned by Dr. Jackie Benton, the American physician I told you about who donated her salary and chose to live without electricity or running water. When I first visited her, she was stroking a honeybee's wings as No Name Creek flowed through her permaculture farm, and she began to share with me her wildcrafter philosophy of living on a planet facing potential catastrophe. I accepted Jackie's offer to stay in her twelve-by-twelve for a season while she traveled. There I befriended her eclectic neighbors—organic farmers, scrap-biofuel brewers, eco-developers—and discovered a beautiful but imperiled way of life.

I share that "Transition" story in its entirety in my book *Twelve by Twelve,* but I want to revisit part of it—the unique way Jackie used material simplicity to gain her own freedom from the Reef—with you now as it relates to the *quinceañera* inflection juncture you're at.

Since you're questioning school and friends, here's more material for your inquiry grist mill: what's the role of *money* in our lives? Jackie got me considering money and leisure and, more specifically, the fact that we exchange something very precious for money—our own energy, the life force itself. Do we want our natural vigor to drain into what a global marketplace dictates, or do we want to channel it toward creative pursuits—like theater and art, in your case—that come from our deepest talents and interests? Though it may seem a bit humdrum to talk about practical ways of creating and stewarding a household economy, it's essential. After all, the material world is indivisible from our inner worlds. Unless we alter our relationship with externals—and this is very tricky because Separation, as we've seen, is built into all facets of material culture—it's difficult to enter the deeper, joyful natural identity we're exploring.

Inspired in part by Jackie, I've spent years scouting ways to weave an unorthodox economy into my own life, gradually making strides toward freeing myself from what some call wage slavery. For example, I "retire" not just at the end of my life but as often as I can *during* my life by interspersing sabbaticals into the journey. During these "creativity sabbaticals," I have followed my bliss as much as the necessity to pay bills. I honed my writing voice during such periods of "moodling": walking along abandoned railroad tracks, bathing in creeks and rivers, listening to crickets and macaws, meditating, reading books, and growing flowers and food. These activities—and *non*-activities—require little money but abundant time. Well before I met Jackie, your grandfather "Pop" taught me an important lesson when I was your age: live within, or preferably below, your means. He had me bus tables at a local restaurant starting at fifteen so that I'd earn my own spending money. And I worked through college, for a portion of my expenses at east—first in a pizza restaurant and then at one of the college's libraries—and also through graduate school, by then in part-time professional positions at the World Bank and World Conservation Union, earning enough to pay off my Stafford Loans, not over a twenty-year period but rather on graduation day itself. Unlike many of my classmates, I didn't have to accept a more lucrative job under pressure to both pay back debt and support myself, freeing me up to choose aid work.

Unfortunately, I forgot my dad's lesson after I graduated from college. Suddenly I had debt on two credit cards and lived from paycheck to paycheck. A close friend handed me Vicki Robin and Joe Dominguez' *Your Money or Your Life*, which shows how we trade our limited hours of life for money, then use that money for things that bring little satisfaction. Their idea is to ratchet down your expenses to a level of "enough"—since both *too little* and *too much* are recipes for unhappiness. As expenses are ratcheted down and savings grow, we have less need to work for money and more free time to focus on what we really love.

Influenced by these ideas, I began tracking every penny that went out of my life in an account book each evening, amazed to find that some forty percent of my expenses were on things that, in the end, weren't worth the exchange of life force. I graphed it over the months, watching the line of expenses go down without any drop in the quality of my lifestyle. I paid off the debts and took a pair of scissors to my credit cards. I wasn't making a bundle as a teacher, nor later as a humanitarian worker and writer, but I always "paid myself first" before paying bills, depositing twenty percent of each paycheck into investments, and teaching myself financial planning online. Over time, I found myself living well below my means, with a buffer to fund renewing creativity sabbaticals.

This was my own experience "way back when," and I know you inhabit a different world where college expenses, for example, continue to skyrocket. But your Pop's lesson still holds about living below your means. I was also impressed about how you applied to several backcountry wilderness programs for this past summer, working late on your essays to achieve a scholarship at the High Mountain Institute. You were accepted into some programs, rejected at a couple, and only got that one scholarship at HMI, so you gravitated there, avoiding expense and debt through applying yourself across a variety of possibilities.

During the pandemic I was interviewed for a podcast in which the journalist asked me about my book *Dispatches from the Sweet Life*: "Can a person live in the world of ambition and achievement and not be *of* it?" he asked. "Or must we all move to Samaipata?"

You've been asking such questions too, in different ways. You love to visit us out on the land—and take part in the "Captain Fantastic thing" that you've quipped I have going on—but you're also going through a city phase and enjoy the grittier, riot-grrrl edge of Santa Cruz.

I'm not suggesting everyone needs to re-village. A household-economy revolution is spreading, for example, through the FIRE trend—*f*inancial *i*ndependence, *r*etire *e*arly. This movement is not just for wealthy professionals. Frugality, savings, and responsible investment, over time, have unfettered hundreds of thousands of voluntary-simplifiers of varying walks of life, from inner-city Detroit's Sisters of the Soil—an African American women's collective—to the fascinating Southeast Asian community that Thai peasant farmer Jon Jandai describes in his popular TEDx talk, "Life Is Easy. Why Do We make It So hard?" Wherever you live, the goal is not necessarily to attain *total* financial independence. Doing even some of the things Jackie and these others suggest is freeing.

Imagine, as you turn fifteen, the radical power of nurturing these kinds of financial independence ideas. These practical perspectives could help you both listen to you inner voice as it guides you to study and pursue acting, and also give you more financial freedom to feel more secure in your choices. It's a perspective that acknowledges the pragmatic concerns of the theater-skeptical dad from your school picnic—*Why not find a solid profession and perform as a hobby?*—but doesn't lock you into the illusion that your only "solid" choice is acquiescing to Separation . . . with its gated communities and groupthink. Even a bit more frugality and financial independence will, I hope, allow you to *ripple.*

But the journalist from the podcast was also asking about ambition and achievement. He went on to say that many people are happy with competition. "I know many journalists, engineers, and lawyers," he said, "who love their work and *want* to work long hours."

It's not ambition itself that's problematic, but whether, as Camus asks, a person is *free* from ambition. It's whether their silent inner voice is in charge or if Separation is secretly at the helm. Especially in this time of general transition after the pandemic and in times of rising fascism, many people—including a lot those journalists, engineers, and lawyers he mentioned—are looking at what's truly important to them within the short lives they've been gifted. A lot of us today are examining *balance,* as in: *Yes, my work is stimulating, and it contributes to others, but what is it that I sacrifice when I spend ten or eleven hours a day doing it?*

When I lead workshops and we talk about underlying values, people often say: "The most important things to me are health and family." I'll then ask if those are really the most important things to them, and they'll insist they are.

"Well, when was the last time you made a homecooked meal?" I might ask. *Too busy*, comes the response. "When was the last time you rang your grandmother?" *Too busy*.

If care is what we really value—care for our health, care for our family and tribe—are we allowing our life energy to flow through the riverbed of these values, or are we instead directing our time into other things . . . ones we've been told are important but that don't accord with what we say we value?

Of course the careers of many of those in the Mind-making class—the cultural creatives who help fashion the today's imagined social order—*are* stimulating. But other questions emerge, ones about whether a given lifestyle is helping shape a sustainable world now. And for our progeny.

We begin to ask, even in the case of the most dynamic, well-paying careers: Is the activity I'm doing today deeply fulfilling in a way that withstands the test of a daily recognition that I will die someday? Is my work deeply gratifying to myself and others, or is it simply engrossing?

Sure, "I love my work," but which aspects of it are enjoyable distractions from my deepest purpose and which aspects are enjoyable expansions into the unified life force?

Nineteen

Roar

Dear Amaya,

With only four days of residency left, the artists and writers seem energized. Feng Mian pointillates stars on her canvass until dawn. Praise poet Michael hand-binds blank books in Maverick, then fills them with his verse. Photographer Jackson Jespersen's camera trap flashes as birds land to feed amid falling leaves. I wonder about the journey those leaves might take.

Maybe some of them will sail into the Lamoille, then drift through the estuary toward the Atlantic Ocean. I follow an oak leaf down the Atlantic coast to Cuba, down past Colombia, to the Brazilian river mouth of the Amazon. At the same instant another leaf, in Bolivia, falls from a yellow-flowering carnival tree in Samaipata, a tree you and Clea climb, and floats down our nameless creek. Love tracks that leaf down the Piray to the Mamoré and Iténez, into the Amazon, until it drifts into the Atlantic, where your leaf nudges mine and we touch.

But everything dissolves before that.

Standing at the Gihon's edges, I see a thousand mud-embedded leaves becoming riverbank. With scissors and paper I've brought from my studio, I craft leaves, writing on one of them: *Ocean.* I drop it into the flow.

Today a visitor to VSC, the writer Nance Van Winkle, offers a craft talk to a dozen residents who have come to hear the breezy-voiced sixty-year-old extol "the merger of text and visual art." She shows slides of Karen Green's sculptures accompanied by the artist's prose, all of it centering on death and mourning. For example, Green's "forgiveness machine" was a heavy, seven-foot-long piece with a vacuum at one end and a shredder at the other, into which people could feed paper on which they'd written what they wanted to be forgiven, or forgive others, for—a way of addressing the past.

As Van Winkle speaks, a sense of serendipity grows in me as I realize who Karen Green is. She's David Foster Wallace's widow. Returning home in southern California that day in 2008, she found Foster Wallace hanging from their patio roof rafter.

I shoot an unreturned glance over to Verity, the Kenyon poet who told us about Foster Wallace's commencement address. Van Winkle explains that Green grieved by writing her book, *Bough Down.*

As she closes her talk, Van Winkle uses an arresting word—*candescence*—and lets it fill the room. "Candescence," she repeats. "When we're told something straight, we turn away. But where there's candescence . . ." she says, her body tilting slightly toward us as her volume drops, ". . . we *lean in* to hear."

Later, in the light of a waning moon candescent on a favorite Gihon waterfall, I think of Foster Wallace: "Life is about simple awareness—awareness of what is so real and essential, so hidden in plain sight all around us, that we have to keep reminding ourselves, over and over—"

This is water, this is water.

I lean in. The falls' voice is Wallace's, reminding us of our core Western affliction: "The constant gnawing thought of having had, and lost, some infinite thing." Could that infinite thing be candescence?

I lean in closer, the liquid roar patiently eroding the imagined dichotomy between "people" and "nature." Eroding Separation.

I remember two years ago when you, Clea, Melissa, and I marched through Santa Cruz with a thousand others, demanding the declaration of a national emergency in Bolivia to stop the millions of acres of Amazon fires exacerbated by growing Chinese and Brazilian agribusiness and global warming. En masse, we chanted: "*Ni soya, ni coca. ¡El bosque no se toca!*"—Neither for soy, nor for coca leaf. Do *not* touch the forest!—Police looked on threateningly as you chanted this, full throated, your voice rippling into the future.

But you've done more than march. I was so proud when, last year, you put your body in front of hundreds of vehicles in Santa Cruz during a civic action to protest a rigged Bolivian presidential election and the government's increasingly anti-*Pachamama* policies. You told me the experience taught you how much sacrifice it takes to shift big systems as—every day for three full weeks—your mom, grandma, you, and some of your neighbors blocked a major avenue near your house.

In the end, your collective roar succeeded: the government stepped down, triggering a new election.

When you asked about my courtship with Melissa, I told you about our mutual love of Bolivia, where we'd both lived for several years before meeting, and also about how Melissa "passed the test" by so beautifully connecting with you. But I've yet to share that the moment I really *knew* Melissa was "the one" was when a policeman clicked handcuffs onto her wrists and pushed her into a paddy wagon.

In September 2011, we were a not-yet-engaged couple. We'd been standing together all morning with three hundred others in "the center zone," a few hundred feet from the White House in Washington, DC, protesting the Keystone XL pipeline, a multi-billion-dollar project to transport Canadian Tar Sands oil across the US to the Gulf of Mexico to be exported globally. The police had megaphoned three warnings that we leave the area. We refused. Then the police cordoned off the space, and it felt real: caged. Should Melissa and I leave the area, we'd be half-nelsoned, stun-gunned, or worse.

Before our arrest, *Energy Insider* had reported that the Keystone pipeline was a done deal. The US State Department would soon sign it into irreversibility. Through lobbying, Keystone Corporation had the government locked into its agenda. But millions of Americans didn't want the project. Farmers didn't want the risk of leaks into their irrigation sources, and Native Americans didn't want it cutting through their reservations. Environmentalists didn't want more fossil fuels horizontally drilled out of Tar Sands and then burned into an already-cooking climate.

Yet it didn't seem there was anything to be done. Mainstream environmental groups were ignored, and Congress wasn't going to oppose the State Department. That's when ordinary citizens decided to revolt.

Over a period of two weeks, *thousands* of us were arrested in the center zone during a civil disobedience action to say "no" to the Keystone pipeline. It caused a splash, especially when many big environmental and social justice organizations with millions of citizen members signed a joint letter saying: "There's not one inch of daylight between our position and those outside getting jailed." Now under real pressure, Hillary Clinton, then Secretary of State, backed off the deal. To this day it remains stalled, and observers credit this victory to the defiance of good-citizen lawbreakers.

Since I'd never been detained, I felt queasy being commanded by police with guns to do something yet refusing to comply. Who wants to be forced to wait, after detention, in the blazing sun for hours with your bladder about to burst and no bathroom available? Who wants to then experience cuffs cinched on tight and being dragged to a barred van? It wasn't fun being driven to a prison on the DC outskirts or seeing fellow protestors jailed for three days even as Melissa and I were released after paying a fine, partly because the system was unable to detain people in such large numbers.

Fun, no. Exhilarating, yes. When the action began, drums beat as hundreds of us marched solemnly toward the White House. I felt the life force surge into me in front of the iconic White House as we—in tribe—disobeyed armed men in an attempt to prevent more fossil fuels being thrown onto climate chaos. A thousand supporters cordoned off from us cheered each time one of us was shackled and led to police vans. When the officer cuffed Melissa, somebody hollered out, "Thank you, good woman!" I felt emotion rise. She and I had talked a lot about marriage, but—in maverick tribe now, with that good woman—I *knew*.

I'm not suggesting you wantonly break the law, but sometimes *roaring*—peacefully defying Separation as part of a community of free humans, as you did in the Santa Cruz roadblocks—can be tactical and personally liberating. It also builds communities of resistance. I like what the late environmentalist Edward Abbey, author of *The Monkey Wrench Gang*, once said with his trademark humor: "Society is like a stew. If you don't stir it up every once in a while, a layer of scum floats to the top. Agitate."

The Keystone civil disobedience that Melissa and I were a part of not only stopped a pipeline. It also helped me and many others deepen inwardly as we raised our collective voice outside of our comfort-decibel-levels. For example, since it could have affected my employment, I worried that my dean at NYU might hear about the arrest. Many people today, looking safely from this side of history, may admire a Martin Luther King Jr., or Mahatma Gandhi for getting arrested, but when you shake up the status quo in your own era, you're often cold-shouldered, whether getting tear-gassed for saying Black Lives Matter or jailed for defending Native rights by obstructing the Dakota Pipeline or pushing back in street protests as the Trump administration guts environmental protections and gives mega-corporations free reign. It's See, Be, Do, again. What do I see *right now*? What do I intuitively feel—within my silent inner acre—that I should *do*?

Do you remember, *hija*, getting choked up when we watched the South Korean fantasy movie *Okja*, about a little girl who tried to save her pet pig from a factory farm? You were maybe twelve at the time, and we viewed it with your friend Ginger during one of your vacations, in the back room of Yaku, a vegetarian restaurant in Samaipata. Afterward, we walked home through the chilly night, the three of us silent, up the hill to our house. By siding with life and defending the pig, the girl in the film bucked the established imagined order and became as expendable as the animal.

If art, as Rene Daumal put it, "is knowledge realized in action," then it's not surprising that maverick artists—those who act to show us the Reef, as Jasmin does, as well as those who swim away from it—are persecuted. As a budding artist, actress, and artisan yourself, it's vital that you know this.

In a previous era that also saw authoritarianism on the rise, Adolf Hitler personally curated the *Entartete Kunst* (Degenerate Art) exhibit in Berlin and then sent as many of the contributing artists to concentration camps as he could. A few years later Senator McCarthy used the Cold War-era House Un-American Activities Committee to imprison hundreds of artists, and also caused actors like Charlie Chaplin, Thomas Mann, and three hundred other actors, authors, and directors to be blacklisted from working in Hollywood, denied work for decades because of unsubstantiated "subversion" charges.

But today, maverick artists face danger. My friend Todd Lester coordinates the nonprofit ArtistSafety, which assists culture workers at risk due to their work; artists like Ai Weiwei, M.F. Husain, Jafar Panahi, and dozens of others. Beyond well-publicized cases like Salmon Rushdie, writers such as Dareen Tatour, a Palestinian poet in northern Israel, and Asl Erdoğan, a novelist in Turkey, are locked up for sharing maverick ideas.

A hundred protestors were recently arrested when they gathered at Trump Tower in Manhattan to demand the release of Mahmoud Khalil, the Palestinian activist who was detained by immigration authorities. This is one of an increasing number of mass arrests as ordinary people push back against the "Trump effect," which is not just at play in the US It's a worldwide backslide on universal human rights, as well as an acceleration of authoritarian practices and corporate greed.

Think also of activist-artists like Sea Shepherds founder and marine conservationist Paul Watson, branded a terrorist by Japanese and Canadian politicians for his direct actions against whale and seal hunters. And recall how, US climate-change activists superglued their chained hands together and to walls and door frames in the Capitol and, because no legislators would acknowledge their concerns, the police removed and jailed them. More than a thousand people were arrested at Extinction Rebellion climate protests in London, in the biggest civil disobedience event in recent British history.

Such underreported current events aren't new. The chaining of the limbs of those who obstruct Separation has been happening for a very long time.

The other day, when I asked VSC cofounder Jon Gregg about the ubiquitous 💮 symbols that adorn the front doors of all Vermont Studio Center buildings, he told me the symbol was proposed by Russian artist Nichola Roerich during World War I. It was intended as an internationally understood symbol to mark museums, schools, and other cultural landmarks. If communities painted the symbol—in red, on their roofs—to alert aerial bomber pilots to their innocence, Roerich suggested, they might avert destruction.

After sharing this history with me, Jon ran his fingers through his curly white beard and added: "Today, the 'Roerich symbol' is about more than just avoiding aerial bombs. It has come to mean safety for artists in times of war *and* in times of apparent peace."

I watch Jasmin work through the Reef hole. Today, she's painting something from Ta-Nehisi Coates on the structure: "The Dreamers plunder not just the bodies of humans, but the body of the Earth itself." I wonder what would happen to mavericks like Jasmin a century from now, in Gaia's time, should they call out what could be an even more Separated civilization— such as the bracomi Domain—than ours is today.

I'd prepared a fruit salad for her in the Mill House kitchen and now pass it through the opening and place it on a table just inside the Reef. Absorbed in work, Jasmin doesn't seem to notice.

My mind goes back to a conversation we had before she'd sealed herself in, one that resonates even more since the pandemic and the ways in which we have begun to reexamine once-standard practices. While we were plastering the Reef together on stepladders, she said: "I think part of why I'm doing this piece is *shame*. It may be why we're having problems back home."

I knew what she meant by *back home*: the intentional community where she lives in Tennessee, a lesbian eco-village that's part of the Land Dykes network spanning dozens of rural communities in the US South in which, as Jasmin put it, "gay women gather and reconnect to each other, to the Earth, and—as much as possible—to surrounding communities." She'd told me her eco-village was fracturing along a chasm between, as she put it, "action-people and process-people": between women who, in effect, enjoy things like governance, agriculture, and so on, and those "who want to spend hours— *days*—processing their emotional issues in a sort of group therapy in our common spaces, or through dance and art."

The sun broke through the clouds outside, and the inside of her sculpture was illuminated in deep gold as light spilled through the windows. Jasmin looked around, squinting, then over at me. "My community isn't some kind of bubble outside reality. We're caught in a civilizational process that goes back to my slave ancestors, but really, it's *everywhere*. One example is this: 'Shave your legs or feel ashamed.' And it extends out into lots of other things. If you don't use deodorant, *shame*.

We need to move through today's dead reef of shame to a world where everyone can be with hair, without hair. With smell, without smell." She laughed.

"With clothes, *without* clothes!" she continued. "We have to make a new culture, decolonizing our minds from capitalist culture and welcoming in a new one which helps us express ourselves in all different ways as we release feelings of shame. We have to be nimble and adjust our thinking. There are so many things that are holding us back as we try to unlearn all this cultural stuff that has filled us with shame and stands in our way."

Now, the memory of this conversation recedes as I watch Jasmin put down her paint brush and walk over to pick up my fruit salad offering. "Thanks," she says, then takes out a scrap of paper, draws a rough sketch on it, and hands it to me.

She's drawn a knife. I ask her what she means, but she's silent. I think I understand the request.

I cross Mill House Bridge, heading toward the VSC kitchen. The other day, I saw a late-middle-aged man strapping his two kids into the back of his minivan while his wife talked on her cell. He had on a T-shirt that read: the hippies were right.

I appreciated the joke. There was a sort of resigned wisdom in the message, suggesting what might have been. After all, the 1960s counterculture, for all of its contradictions, could have *become the culture*. Or at least altered it more profoundly. The "60s generation's" mass rebellion against the status quo included tens of millions of people, most of them young. Much analysis exists on the reasons the movement fell short of truly renewing our culture, but it's worth considering that what happened once can happen again. That latent energy bubbles up to the surface in brave, new times, and I wonder about you, a Powers Cortez, a biracial participant in a BIPOC (Black, Indigenous, People of Color) generation rising up in so many ways. I consider the ways you and your friends are "maladjusted to empire" in high school today, then think of you on a US campus in a couple of years during, perhaps, a Roaring Twenties of a new—and ancient—roar.

I arrive at the kitchen and select a serrated knife. Holding it in my hand, I think back to that rainy night in Queens and feel conflicted about giving it to Jasmin. Though I don't know her intentions, I trust my friend.

When I arrive at her studio with the knife, Jasmin is visible through the Reef cavity. Passing the sharp implement through handle first, I speak words to her that were once directed at Melissa when the police cuffed her: "Thank you, good woman."

With a nod, the maverick artist accepts the knife and my words. She squeezes my hand as if to reassure me, and I search her eyes for clues.

Twenty

Rippling Further

Gaia's Seed

Chapter Three– March 30th, 2139

(Eight years later. Southern Pacific Ocean, six-hundred kilometers from Lima, Peru.)

Dear Calder,

Gazing over empty ocean, I'm not surprised this day has come. My last. I've been preparing for it for months. Although your dad's tried his best to thwart Asia Domain from mastering our ship, they've been narrowing in on our location by the week. Now we're pinned.

Memories sail with me, son. Memories of land. Like that morning when you were five, when I woke up after sleeping beside you on the second-floor mezzanine bed over our kitchen. Do you remember? Your dad was still sleeping next to Julia in her room. When I looked down from the bed you were already up, sitting in the nook at our breakfast table. Your face tilted skyward, you seemed to be contemplating the raindrops on the skylight. The rain had fallen in darkness, and it bejeweled the glass above. You swallowed a mouthful of peach, regarding the beauty that remained of night rain.

Rapt as you were, Calder, you could not have seen the other marvel behind you: Out the kitchen window glistened orange cosmos, purple morning glories, and yellow sunflowers declaring: Everything, everything, *everything* is waiting for you.

Later that same day, you went outside and collected dozens of acorns which had fallen with the night rain and placed them out to dry in a straight row on our south-facing balcony. You know that I kept them. At the time, it seemed a bit silly to jar the acorns along with our other seeds. I labeled the vessel "oak" and set it on a dusty workshop shelf amid the seeds of useful things like bottleneck squash and Bolivian persimmon, peach and heritage tomatoes. I carried the oak jar along when we evacuated to Citadel eight years ago and brought it aboard. Today, I poured the remaining acorns into my and Jim's pockets, and, in a little while, we'll launch them toward Peru. Genetic messages in earthen bottles.

Only a dozen acorns remain. Two months ago, your dad and I planted some on a rooftop farm in Santiago. We'd docked off the Chilean city and spent ten days at the apartment of a Settler friend from back in Johnson— you may remember Lizzy Guzman. She now lives beneath the farm. I gardened with fervor in Santiago, my shirt sweat soaked, hands covered with soil, weeding the pea rows of "Pachamama," the name for the planet's largest human rooftop soil farm. After years at sea, touching earth again. From Lizzy's two acres of cropland atop the *Edificio Imperio* in the Bellas Artes district, the big-sky view astonished me, Santiago's skyline and the Pacific agleam. Up on Pachamama, one forgets the bracomi commerce below.

On my first morning there, carrying a bucket of weeds to the compost pile, I glanced over to the far side of the aerial grange and saw Lizzy's petite silhouette as she directed a work crew. Our old friend is forty now, her thick brown hair down to her waist. In 2136, Lizzy cofounded Pachamama along with Gwen Flanner, a devolved bracomi from Valparaiso. Previous to the pair's arrival, a Bridger team had stealthed five square blocks around *Edificio Imperio*. It was dodgy to do back then because nobody knew if "Pachamama," among our first costal city pilot efforts, could be masered. Lizzy and Gwen went to work fitting the roof with a thick, plastic root barrier, craning up thousands of soil sacks and shaping earth into rows studded with tomato seedlings and chard plugs. *Y así* a farm took shape.

I wish you could have seen it, Calder. The farm's green-roof system holds 1.8 million pounds of loam—the 1947 building is verified to bear the weight. The soil is a special mix of compost and porous stones, which eases the load, and in it grows organic produce for visiting ships. Several seasons in, Pachamama has expanded to a new roof a block away. Planting corn together one afternoon, Lizzy enthused about how—someday, as humans ripple out to the frontier—farmers markets and restaurants will get ultra-fresh, subway-delivered produce with a zero-transport footprint. "This is just the kernel of the future green city," she said, "where a single, lightweight, eight-story tower of recycled materials could supply produce for fifty thousand people through organic hydroponics on each floor."

Hijo, who could have predicted humans could seize city blocks so swiftly? Tell the pessimists on your liner about Santiago. Your dad and I heard about your community's riff from your *tío*. He messaged us that one of your crew, an officer at that, was overheard grumbling: "In the end, nothing matters. A species lives and it dies, and that's it."

It's infectious, because he now has others bandying the word "extinction" about. I can't say such naysayers are outright wrong. When they look at the math, they see the glass as half empty. Only twenty million humans remain in the world. If you put that figure next to over one billion bracomis, our extermination can seem logical. These "realists" also point to bracomi atrocities against our most vulnerable minority, the hundred thousand or so iconoclast land-humans sticking it out in what amounts to hunter-gatherer bands. Living in caves and trees on several continents, they steal into the open only at night but are nonetheless picked off steadily.

You can also, however, see the glass as half full, with the water rising. While it's true that the Domain, a few years back, masered our global flotilla down to just four thousand ships, human tech improvements have today increased our fleet to ten thousand, and rising. Add to that our covert city blocks, plus more islands around the world than I can count. Mere *humans* are doing this, hijo. You were probably too young to remember our motto back in Johnson: *If you don't think the little guy can make a difference, try spending the night in a room with a few mosquitoes*. That's us.

Even so, you're bound to feel despair now and then. There isn't a human alive who hasn't felt symptoms of extinction neurosis, but when E.N. reefs you in (and it will), take strength in your name, *Calder*. Your dad and I had planned to share your name's deeper meaning during your *quince* initiation, but I'll tell you in this letter. Allow me to gather the words.

I'm crying now. I miss you. You're my precious seed. You grew in a womb I'd been programmed to forget, until your dad led me across the river to my mislaid memory. You and Julia are the seeds of our species' survival. But no pressure, honey. :)

Your dad is next to me now, also writing to you. We just finished our letters to Julia. When we complete yours, he'll droog them off. Your sister, on *tía*'s ship, has just entered into the Bay of Bengal. When your dad first suggested, two years ago, that we separate our family, I protested. But today I'm beyond grateful for his foresight: disperse your spores and some will blow into the future.

Very early in my pregnancy with you, your dad said to me one afternoon: "I think I hear something."

We were in our Johnson living room, and he had his ear squished onto my belly. I tousled his hair and whispered: "Not yet, Jim."

But you became audible to us the following week when the midwife brought a sonogram machine to our farm-in-training. We heard a pinhead heartbeat, and I saw a grainy image of you. That evening, Jim quit his habitual nightly dram of hard cider and joined me in a "ghost pregnancy," announcing he'd go booze free with me during a forty-day couple's meditation. Every evening, we sat cross legged and back to back and sang a two-octave mantra as you grew.

Here's a sweet thing I'm thinking about during my last hours of life: Jim and I have started up "your" couple's mediation again! It began a month ago on Rapa Nui.

Easter Island. We docked there after Santiago, for five days, the maximum safe period we'd estimated. Rooftop "Pachamama" was nothing compared to the real thing. We spent those precious days hiking dunes and woods and exploring the long-abandoned Moai stone statues which are surrounded today by a Citadel-type eco-village where hundreds of Settlers live in treehouses, "cob-igloos," and twelve-by-twelve, post-and-beam homes.

Granted, we had to hide from sundown to sunup because of a temporary curfew, and we were issued a cramped third-floor studio in Hanga Roaa that smelled of mildew. And yet, shiplike as our restricted quarters were, a gorgeous *tree* sheltered our building. We'd sit beside our sole window, not outside but still under the tree's canopy, meditating morning and night just like we did when you were in my belly.

"*Mira!*" your dad cried out after our mediation the first morning there. Just outside our window, atop a wrought-iron fire escape beneath the tree's canopy, perched two adorable puffballs: baby mourning doves, looking almost ready to leap!

We watched the baby doves each day on Rapa Nui, the pair of fluffy dandelion-seed heads bobbing side by side. The chicks bounced softly between the fire escape and a tree bough. When the wind blew, they swayed with the tree, sticking to the stretch of branches above the fire escape. Every so often Mama Dove swooped in to alight beside her babies. Seeing her, they'd instantly switch from cottony composure to noisy wing flapping, stabbing their beaks into Mom's mouth for her gourmet regurgitation. I felt a stab of remembrance of you and Julia as ravenous fledglings.

Your dad designated two old seat covers for dove-viewing breakfasts, and each morning we'd clamber onto the building's roof postmeditation and eat tough bread and the daily fruit rationed to us. Pelicans flew over too, and we'd watch small flocks of them merge, disconnect, then reconnect as we talked about how we'd love to join the pioneers on Rapa Nui. We anguished over it. But in the end knew we couldn't return to land. Not yet. The *Wu Wei*'s work was pollination: assisting other vessels and transferring code through Jim and our ship's other Bridgers. We were also on the cutting edge of Memory.

Calder, as you may be gleaning from your *tío*, this is our species' most important long-term mission.

We are a minority prey species, so we can't face the majority bracomi predator in the open. Yet nor can we increase our numbers through good stealth alone. The new tech you'll explore—should you Bridge after your *quince* celebration, rising to sub-Captain—will open up a world now unimaginable to you. You'll delve into how we humans, as Bridgers, can now do much more than stealth major island-sized landmasses. We've come to operate . . . *within bracomi memory*.

This isn't a one-off job. We have to fluid, radiate, and otherwise hack into them thousands of Alzheimer's blind spots, strains of vertigo, and related bugs every minute. I'm oversimplifying things as much as I can; humans can't comprehend speeds approaching infinity. The bracomis, of course, cure our Bridger viruses nearly as fast as we create them, but not quite as fast. As the pesky mosquitoes in the room, we've got it to the point where human existence in the world feels uncertain to the vast majority of bracomis. It's as if we're a dream they had last night, and one that's forever dissipating. Or you could say that almost all of the bracomis sleepwalk around us. *Almost* all of them.

I'm pretty sure you've guessed what's happening. My maternal instinct was to ease into this for your benefit, and you know how "Mom overshares," as you used to joke, especially when there's much to process. When I devolved, I discovered speech, and then the speaking never stopped! Oh, Calder, I'm all over the place, but how can a mother break this kind of news to her son? Two heavy pistons sit on deck beside your dad and me as our feet dangle over the helm. In an hour, at sunset, we'll strap these pistons to our torsos.

Right now, I'm taking in the awful sight of Jaime and Balu wrapping up together in a barnacled anchor chain. And Thiago is portside with his two best buddies, filling his pockets with fishing sinkers and hand tools. We're all doing whatever it takes to get heavy. Most of us have decided to swallow thesplale just before sinking in order to die instantly at water contact, but your father and I are choosing to dive without the drug.

A few of our *Wu Wei* crew are already sinking, maybe already on ocean bottom. We're masered and estimate the bot subs will arrive in two hours. Our choice is the same one faced by countless other masered ships: capture by bracomis or euthanasia.

A Honduran trawler, the *Living Bridge,* that was docked beside us in Santiago didn't have that choice. After we departed Chile, bracomis surprised the *Living Bridge* and vamped the crew's biodata before Eliminating them. That's how they found us. They can harvest data even after a human's death, so, to escape the Domain's reach, we're forced to the ocean bottom.

You need to know something very important: despite all of this, your mom isn't scared.

Wow. I stopped writing for a second, to stem my crying, and I realized that mine are tears of joy. Joy because you and Julia are safe. Joy at the life I've had with your dad. But mostly: *joy*, period. The difference, *hijo*, between three additional hours and three additional decades of life is minor compared to how a human being chooses to live right now. The most vital thing I've learned during years captive on the *Wu Wei* is that joy is my base state. The bracomi can't injure me; that's my own job. Refuse the job of harming myself, and I'm free. Free to connect to who I am: the immeasurable, indestructible energy of life itself. After sunset, I'll continue to be the ocean I've always been.

I don't fault the bracomis for our situation. Nor do I blame our ancestors, a century back, for willingly chipping themselves because they were so lost that they couldn't hear the Earth whispering to them all along in sunflowers, low tides, and falling leaves. I do look back to the past—I'm human, after all!—but it's with melancholic gratitude for the honest rebel lives lived by millions who resisted back in Cusp times and merged with humus beneath unvisited graves. If not for the consciousness of these anonymous millions, our situation would be far worse. There might no longer be words.

Some suicide note, eh son? I just bounced that line off your dad to see if it's too much. "Leave it in," he said with the faux tough-guy smirk you know. "Calder's a man."

What I mean, son, is that *we've got time, even now*. Even here, there is no urgency. These letters to you and you sister are part of a calm wrap-up to a good life. Your dad and I have lived well. And truthfully. For us, that's enough. We just side-armed, one by one, our final acorns out to ocean, each with a wish for you and Julia. We have no illusion they'll reach the shore and bear. Like ourselves, they'll dissolve into ocean. The ripples they create as we throw them don't go anywhere or affect anything. Or do they?

While dove-watching back on Rapa Nui, your dad and I brainstormed a list of books we'd love for you and Julia to read someday. He mentioned Edward Abbey's *The Monkey Wrench Gang*–fun!–and Saul Alinsky's *Rules for Radicals*, which is as pertinent now as ever.

I included your great-*times-three*-granddad's volume, *Ripple*. That book is why, as a bracomi, I devolved into the Vermont Studio Center simulation. All of us "VSC artists" were tracing our roots by channeling dead artist relatives. My "authentic heritage experience" was to reenact the pre-Cusp residency of my DNA-great-great-grandfather. *Ripple* was one of a thousand banned books from Cusp times that humans, and devolving bracomis too, read anyway, probably precisely because they were banned. Reading itself came to be the ultimate dissident act. It made us slow down from warp speed to *el buen ritmo*. A good speed.

We humans, today, create our new reality through meditation and group visualization. The islands and roof-top farms we now settle began in our imaginations! Over the past months, through on-deck meditations on thousands of ships, we've been doing a collective visualization: we'll retake a whole continent. Australia.

Every day, in our minds, we drink fresh water from Australian streams and plant oak trees for shade, creating the kind of balanced human culture where we can pick fruit off the trees as we walk the landscape. And all of this is done through acceptance of something vital. It's probably the most important thing I have to say to you, Calder, before I go. It is this: in the deepest sense, we are *all* bracomi.

The defensive aspect of Memory, however adroitly we may hack bracomi programming and camouflage ourselves, is patchwork and partial. In Domain-speak, these tactics win thousands of battles a second, but only stalemate the war. You'll soon learn, *hijo*, about our long-term Memory strategy, a multigenerational process to change, simultaneously, bracomi programming *and* our own.

For it would be foolish of us to think: "We created the bracomis, so now we'll destroy them." They aren't Frankensteins we cooked up in a lab. There is no enemy out there because *we ourselves became bracomis* by doing daily visualizations of another sort: subconscious visualizations woven a century ago into the original fiction of the Separated collective order. Humans a hundred years ago imagined themselves, every day, as entities *separate* from "nature" and "the cosmos" . . . and that's how they gradually manifested themselves as bracomi.

Do you see where Mom is going with this, Calder? Your role, as you turn fifteen and cross into adulthood, will be to help shift the narrative. As long as bracomis-humans (it's one word, really) still believe the superiority story— *We're the pinnacle of evolution; We're a thousand times smarter than Primitives*—we'll retake Australia only to tire of it and then decide to "Evolve" into some other variety of bracomi.

Your journey, one imposed by survival, will not be easy. So my wish for you is that the name your father and I gave you is a touchstone for the strength you'll need.

Calder, in rugged pagan English, means "Rough Waters."

The ones I crossed when your dad reached across the Gihon. The ones you, your sister, and your *tíos* now sail together in tribe. The ones that will bring you, someday, to our first continent, perhaps to the banks of a strange and powerful river.

How I burn to say to you: *I'll see you downriver, son.* But that would be fantasy. Take it from an ex-borg who's stretched to the outer edges of science: there is no blissful afterlife where I'll get to gaze, once more, into your eyes. Nor will you, in some sweet hereafter, be able to hug Mom again. You're an orphan now, Calder, but we'll always be together because the waters, my love, are one.

Twenty-one

Living Bridge

Dear Amaya,

Several acorns bump up alongside me today as I swim the Gihon. I snatch them from the flow. As I dry off in the late morning sun, I scan the upriver tree canopy for an oak that might have dropped them, but I see none.

I arrange the acorns in a row beside my towel to dry, then lay back, close my eyes, and listen to the river whisper. After a time, I rise, pocket the acorns, and walk downriver to the place where the mega-storm leveled the bridge. Four mossy concrete pillars remain, along with bits of the oak pylons that once rose here. Climate change took the rest. Walking these ruins, I think of Jasmin. Her studio was silent this morning, unusually so. I make a mental note to check in on her.

Today's my final day in Vermont, *hija*. This morning before the swim, I walked to the thrift shop behind the United Church of Johnson to look for clothes for you and Clea. Sizing up blouses and jeans against a college-student employee, I marveled at your adult dimensions. I bought a big suitcase, too, and loaded it with the used clothing, gifts, and Hawaiian leis for a possible fun detail for your *quinceañera* celebration. Then I headed down Main Street for Morrisville maple syrup, finally climbing to my attic room to stash the gatherings. Out the clerestory window, the Gihon bubbled west to the Atlantic Ocean, pulling me toward you, and I reread your beautiful text from the previous day:

> Daddy, Gaia's so brave. Even going to her death, she's just so . . . *no sé*. I told you by the river that day:"You live and you die and that's it." But Gaia inspires me with something different. I think it's more like, "You live and you create and that's love." But I do NOT accept the ending! She should not have to commit suicide in the ocean someday. She's MY great-granddaughter!! :) And I'm going to re-write her story. Stay tuned, because I've already started thinking about another possible Gaia.

At the site of the collapsed bridge, I listen. I write and brush watercolor into my notebook, thinking of you rewriting Gaia's story. Yours and mine are tributary tales, tiny trickles along a human frontier of riot grrrls and Reef-sculptors, Transition innovators and workaday urban mavericks. Could such droplets someday—some*how*—become a fulsome part of the enormous river where the Story of Separation so forcefully flows?

I remember, as the pandemic peaked, seeing Bill Gates on the news promoting his book on confronting climate change. "It's true that my carbon footprint is absurdly high," he was saying. "I own big houses and fly in private planes—in fact, I took one to Paris for the climate conference—so who am I to lecture anyone on climate change?" Yet that major CNN show, and many like it, provided the billionaire wide berth to promote a high-tech climate vision to a billion viewers worldwide. In the interview, Gates didn't talk much about challenging the *underlying* causes of climate change or modifying his own lifestyle. Instead, he shared costly for-profit carbon fixes—like corporate cloud-seeding and UV-defection mirrors and ocean methane-capture-tech—which promise a utopic Earth able to absorb more footprints the size of his own: 7,493 metric tons last year. (Compare that, *hija*, to the average annual American carbon footprint of sixteen metric tons, or the average world citizen's footprint: four metric tons.)

The same week as the Gates interview, the nonprofit Oxfam International had released a major report on climate and inequality, but it didn't make it onto CNN. Only a few of us would happen to see the Oxfam report and learn that the wealthiest 1 percent of the global population have used twice as much carbon as the poorest 50 percent over the past twenty-five years. Few outlets covered the findings about how, in the year 2020 alone, billionaires' wealth increased by $4 trillion, while the number of people living on less than six dollars a day increased to five hundred million.

These inequalities extend out to carbon: during the commercial-travel bans of Covid times, for example, private jet sales soared. "In country after country," Oxfam noted, "it is the richest who are least affected by global economic crisis and are the quickest to see their fortunes recover. They also remain the greatest emitters of carbon and the greatest drivers of climate breakdown." Meanwhile, the most vulnerable humans absorb the pain of climate change, as inconsistent rainfall and new pests harm their crops, resulting in hunger and displacement from ancestral lands.

With bare hands, I dig into the warm, dark humus—the pure organic mulch of decades of falling leaves—around the former bridge for an idea I've dreamed up. Then I watercolor and let fall a fresh leaf: *Bracomis and Humans are One* rides the watercourse. While I acknowledge the accuracy of reports like Oxfam's, I don't blame anyone as the report implicit does. Separation is systemic, not personal. Even the CEOs of logging multinationals clearcutting the jungle have to go home at night and read their children stories of happy forest animals.

Thinking of you, I drop this in the river: *Today's world is Separated*. Then I try to reorder the letters> *Water adds a lost poetry*. This anagram is still two letters off; your turn.

It's almost noon when I see the boy. The one I told you about, whose dad told him: "Don't step in the water." The boy's face is red, as if he might have been crying, but he also wears a captivated look as he picks up rocks, throws them one by one into the Gihon, and watches the still water shatter.

Surprised to see him this far from town, I scan for the adult who must be here. I spy his mom above him on the far embankment, and we exchange waves. To the boy, I'm a familiar face. He and I have nodded to each other during my walks past his duplex, on my way to Maverick. Now he's directly across the river from me, just forty feet away. For each rock he chucks, I toss an acorn into the flow, and it becomes a game. Eventually, he half-smiles. My feet are bare, and I step into the river. He takes his flip-flops off. And he steps in too.

His mom smiles and shakes her head, but doesn't tell him not to.

After the boy is gone, I gaze into a river that does what words would love to do—find form by constantly vanishing.

Games played out, the Gihon is glassier than I've ever seen it, a crystalline pane that magnifies flashing minnows and smooth pebbles. I squint into this liquid lens, to maybe gaze through a membrane into subterranean aquifers. Then I close my eyes and feel the water meander through my inner acre's shadows.

Do you remember that warm December evening in Samaipata when I asked you: "Heard of the Grateful Dead?"

It was your summer break between fourth and fifth grade. Melissa and I had recently moved to Bolivia full time, and were still adapting to the upside-down-world feeling of a summer Christmas. The previous day, you'd watched Clea take her first steps. "The *what*?" you answered, looking up from the book you were reading in the hammock.

"Mmm . . . '*los muertos agradecidos*,'" I said, fumbling to translate the name of a band totally unknown in Bolivia.

You cocked your head and frowned cutely. For the previous few days, the Grateful Dead's "Box of Rain" had been stuck in my head, partly because it had been intermittently drizzling. You and I had worn rain ponchos as we visited your friends and traveled the wild-dog trails on our land. Part of why I like the song is the mystery it holds: I don't quite know *what* a "box of rain" *is*.

There's a similar sweet ambiguity with the song "Ripple," in which Jerry Garcia sings: "Let it be known there is a fountain / that was not made by the hands of men." The two songs capture a state of melancholy, transience, and connection to the life force that I relate to. I played "Ripple" for you, and "Box of Rain," and the rest of the 1970 album *American Beauty*. You listened while you read.

Later, I asked you what you thought of the album. "It's fine," you said, looking at me sleepily, blankly.

"I saw the Dead live one time. In Madison Square Garden," I said. "I was in high school . . . 1988." I realized you were adrift. Your cultural reference points were *cuñapé* pastries and the band *Los Kjarkas*, the Santa Cruz plaza and reggaeton.

"You saw the Dead . . . *live*?" you finally said, forcing an ironic smirk through your sleepy face.

The next morning, while you, Clea, Melissa, and I were Skyping with your *tía* Amy's family in Vermont, I said to your *tío*: "We thought of you last night, Andrew. Amaya listened to the Grateful Dead for the first time."

"Which album?"

I told him it was *American Beauty*. He nodded: "Good place to start."

Over *tío* Andrew's shoulder, snow fell. In Samaipata it was eighty plus, and a bikini-clad Melissa had said to me that morning, by the Cuevas waterfalls, "I know I should feel nothing but gratitude. So why do I miss a piney scent and the chance of snow?" I peered through pixels into a familiar life: your *tíos*' family living room, the toy shelf, the wood-burning stove, the ice-slicked solar panels out the window, and the boulder down by the creek that your cousins dubbed "Big Rock Candy Mountain" after the Harry McClintock folk song about a hobo's humorous idea of paradise, a landscape filled with lakes of gin and cigarette trees. In the toned-down kids' version your cousins sing in their dome, Big Rock Candy Mountain is the place where "it's Christmas every day." The stockings hung on the mantle, the decorated tree. A frost-sparkling New England through the window.

Back then, Melissa and I felt the wistfulness of our leave-taking from kin and birthplace. We'd chosen to re-tribe, but not into new visions of "American beauty" alongside your *tíos*. You probably know that I'm sharing this memory with you now because I feel once again—even as I yearn to rejoin you, Melissa, and Clea on our Samaipata acres—a migrant's melancholy over leaving tomorrow. Vermont is my native habitat, or close to it. The oaks, birch, and pines (so different from Samaipata's "exotic" pacay, eucalyptus, and guapuru) are the trees of the Nassakeag swamp forest of my youth. The Gihon's banks are nearly identical to those of the Nissequogue River near my childhood home. I grew up suburban, but it wasn't completely Separated. It was *this*, too: these honeysuckle scents of late June, a river's gurgle, croaking frogs, all in a place where—unlike in Samaipata—it *snows*. I remember Mrs. Meyers, my first-grade public school teacher on Long Island, on an early-winter morning when she must have noticed the season's first snowflakes falling out the window. "Kids, put down your pencils," she said, impulsively, as if seized. "We're going outside to catch snowflakes on our tongues."

Just like that. I recall my complete surprise: what an anomaly in our routines of lining up to walk the halls under florescent lights and sitting quietly at a desk. Just like that, we all put on coats and shuffled through the back door of our classroom into the December chill. I pointed my little face upward.

Snowflakes fell on my nose and my cheeks. They tickled. I looked around: twenty other faces pointed into falling wonder. Soon I caught one on my tongue, and then another and another. I was the last kid out there. Mrs. Meyers had to call out, firmly: "*Billy!*" Chilled to the bone, I took my seat in a classroom that felt . . . different.

The poet Michael will return to Baltimore tomorrow. Raghu will fly in the morning to Vancouver to read from *The Farthest Field*. And Feng Mian.

She's beside me now, looking over the edge of the Mill House Bridge into the Gihon's sparkling blue. She tells me she's finished her stars. "What took me a month to paint is only a fraction of just one galaxy."

Feng Mian looks skyward and I follow her gaze up. "I came here because my country has crazy ideas too," she says. "Like yours, China wants to conquer everything. The ocean floors and rainforests, cyberspace and *outer space*. I wanted to appreciate space through art. Not to colonize Mars and mine asteroids."

Last night, I saw Feng Mian's pair of eight-by-eight-foot canvasses. Finished now, they were displayed in the VSC Open Studios tour for residents and community to view work. I paused before her ten thousand silent white dots. So serene, yet the stars are constantly changing as the universe expands.

"Coming back 'from space'—finishing my paintings—I saw the world anew," Feng Mian tells me. "It's lonely out there, and frigid, even if it's peaceful and beautiful. We only have *this*."

We both watch the river as a delivery truck trundles by. A trio of artists laughs on the far side of the bridge. Feng Mian and I don't speak. Her words and art bring to mind the famed "fleck" image that Hubble took of Earth. Just before the space station left our solar system, astrophysicist Carl Sagan requested that the unmanned Hubble snap one last image of our neighborhood—a sun and eight planets—before leaving forever. That image gave us a revolutionary picture of ourselves: Earth as a seemingly trivial, colorless speckle. Without even departing our own solar system, within a Milky Way of a hundred billion stars, Earth appears as, well, almost nothing. In the photo, astronomers had to insert an arrow so you'd even notice it.

This fleck, the planet that birthed all of us, is the sole location in infinity where we're sure our species can thrive. It's that precious.

I imagine putting the space station into reverse, turning 180 degrees to power *back* toward the fleck. Would not the most exquisite of faces slowly come into view? A face which, as Feng Mian reminds me today, we've all but forgotten, a luminous countenance that's blue. Rainclouds highlight the azure expression of humanity's own face, the face of Gaia.

The other day, Jasmin passed a color photo to me through the hole in the Reef. She'd scrawled on it: "This is a living bridge."

I examined the photo of a fifty-foot bridge crossing a river. The bridge wasn't made of concrete or steel. The roots of several trees on either side of the water had been woven together over many years, trained to intermingle with those from the other side. This extended braiding process created a functional overpass. In the picture, two teenagers about your age were crossing the *jing kieng jri*, or living bridge.

Researching it, I learned that residents of the northern Indian Meghalaya region have merged *ficus elastica* tree roots over generations into a hundred bridges—the longest one is an amazing 160 feet in length. Today, the structures are at once robust and supple. Even a Frankenstorm can't dislocate them. When we cooperate with the rest of creation, living bridges support our species' passage.

On my way to check in on Jasmin, I notice that something's changed in her studio. From the Mill House parking lot, I see clouds of dust puff out her distant window. I hear a faint sawing sound. Hurrying over, I climb the stairs to spot a shaft of sunlight streaming through the reopened door. Inside, Jasmin uses the knife I gave her to sever the Reef.

I retrace my steps and find saws in the wood shop, then gather a few artists. Together we pull down chunks of the Reef. Some Johnson horticulture-club volunteers, whom I'd met at Karaoke Night, join us too. (I'd recruited them earlier for a final surprise that we're to create together tomorrow morning, Amaya.) Working collectively, along with a good dosage of laughter, it's not long before we topple the Reef. Down to the riverbank, we carry its bones.

Another artist is already there, piling the dismantled scraps of plywood sculpture she'd made from construction-site dumpster materials. Her month's work is now to be tinder at the farewell bonfire tonight. Although most of this month's art—sculptures and watercolors, poems and chapters of novels—will travel to distant homes and galleries, a portion of what we've generated will burn.

At dinner, Jasmin beams joy but doesn't speak. Soon the sun starts to set behind the mountains, and the scent of smoke comes through the window. Somebody's lit the fire.

A group of us heads down to the river, to the sight of small licks of flame. The sun smolders over the Gihon as more artists and community friends arrive. Nobody touches the mountain of Reef residue. We start with the plywood, and an imagined material world begins to burn.

I ask Jasmin what happened at the end, up inside her installation. She's silent, the fire crackling. Then the sculptor says in a low voice: "It's not that I gave up on facing dying corals, or our shame. It was something small that happened shortly before I handed you the sketch of a knife."

The Gihon shimmers, and the setting sun gathers in intensity around Jasmin. "I looked out the window, from where I stood inside the Reef. And I saw a beautiful world. A world just inches away."

I let this pool inside me: *wonder and intimacy, just inches beyond Separation.* The scent of burning pine reminds me of childhood campfires by the Nissocuague. But as much as I've connected with Jasmin and Feng Mian, with the Gihon and the Green Mountains, I know I need to burn my nostalgia for "coming back" to a fictional past. The "living bridge" isn't about living in the past. Remain in the same house for eighty years and you're a migrant anyway, a migrant in time, as the kids on your block grow up and leave, the elders pass away, the woods are felled for development, and FOR SALE signs go up and come down. But nor does a "living bridge" mean living in the future, by either worshiping progress toward better days or fearing what's to come. Past and future are what hold each end of the living bridge in Earth, as all creation crosses an ephemeral present.

When I called Melissa today, she and your sister were out gardening, pulling up "a huge carrot and surprise tomatoes"— ones that I had planted months back. Hands I love dug into humus, the familiar sounds of the town below, the arching sky over Amboró National Park to the north, the San Juan valley to the south and to the west the rise of Cerro La Patria. The adobe house we dreamed up together and built. Your persimmon and Clea's peach, and the hundreds of other trees we've reforested.

And I imagine Clea, when I return, racing—with you and me close behind her—toward the nameless tributary that runs through our land, and together we'll tear off our shoes to *wawawaaa*. Though I cherish your Giggi and Pop, and your *tíos* downstream, I won't linger here out of love of the past. I live now in a flow called home, where the Andes meets the Amazon, with you, Clea, Melissa, and our community.

〰〰〰〰〰〰〰〰〰〰〰〰〰〰〰〰〰

During both routine and transition times in your life whether through chosen re-tribing, unintended displacement, or simply as a result of time's passings you might try a mirror contemplation to remind yourself of the multi-faceted, migrant nature of your own existence.

Steady your face in front of a mirror. Try to see all
the faces—your infant face, child face, current and
future faces, even traces of your ancestors' faces—
flickering under the crystalline surface of your gaze.
Imagine your face, and your very *self* and existence,
as a kind of river which keeps flowing even as
different scenes play out on and below its surface.

Can you delight in your current form, but with an
underlying sense of the deeper, always changing
flow of your existence?

Jasmin picks up a piece of the Reef. To hoots and cheers she
tosses it onto the fire. Others follow, and soon the flames
spring skyward. I join in, pitching pieces into the blaze.

I take out the remaining paper leaves with their watercolor,
the ones not yet launched downriver to you. One by one I
drop them into the flames. So-called "negative" concepts like
The Reef and *Separation* burn just as brightly as "positive" ones like *Biophilia* and *Transition*. Notions ignite,
the words crinkling into ash. Temporary signposts on the
journey, not the destination.

Later that evening, nearly everything torched, Jasmin
stands and picks up the cool end of one of the few still-glowing
Reef chunks. She takes it down to the Gihon.

I rise with her, as do others, and together we collect the
smoldering remains of what had imprisoned her just this
morning, and we begin to place them into the river. Art is a
living bridge, not something monumental and immortal you
can't tear down. It's the immutable spirit of the human, and

that's what's released tonight. Our human tributary—one of thousands of evolving tribes—lobs the Reef's final cinders into the flow. These embers protest through spits and hisses upon contact with the water. But the enduring river takes everything into itself and streams toward ocean.

The following morning a dozen of us gather at the spot where the storm destroyed the bridge.

Jasmin has joined us, as has the poet Michael, and also Terry and Jeff, whose homes I'd help sandbag before the storm. None of them know about my surprise. But the horticulture volunteers do: when we arrive, they've already begun digging. I, too, grab a shovel and press it into the Gihon's bank. Two teenagers trowel holes on the far bank, and Michael places into one of them a drought- and frost-resistant ficus tree sapling. The volunteers brought a dozen of them along to plant. These trees should grow well here, even with little maintenance, so that their roots can eventually braid together over the Gihon.

Jasmin chuckles as she brings a black-bagged treelet over to the hole I've finished. This adaptation of a Meghalaya living bridge, I admit to her, may not flourish here. It depends upon an uncertain climate and good people to steward the trees after we're gone.

"Even if it survives," Jasmin says, as she tucks her sapling into humus, "this bridge won't be completed in our lifetimes."

Exactly, I think, as a leaf cartwheels from an upstream maple. Kissing water, it dimples the flow.

Twenty-two

Seeds Dream Deep

You're back from Vermont!! I can't wait to come and celebrate my *quinceañera* in Samaipata! I've already sent the invitations. Tell me about the *minga* work party. Was Lukka there? How's my persimmon?

Dear Amaya,

We've been eating the delicious fruits of your thriving persimmon tree, and I wish you could have been here to taste them. (Don't worry, I froze some for smoothies.) We're pleasantly anxious about your celebration. Melissa's got the menu down; Clea's helping to pick out the salsa music.

The *minga* was amazing. We spent all of yesterday in our orchard working with what we still fondly call a "pod" of twenty friends. Yes, Lukka was there with his mom, and also our Cochabamba-transplant neighbor Maximo, who raises bees. In the morning, Maximo showed a clutch of us an incredible way to mix manure, black dirt, and sand to create super soil, while another group pruned guava, fig, and pomegranate trees.

In the afternoon, muscles sore and blistered, I stepped away from our work pod for a solo break. Relinquishing the machete I'd been using to clear an invasion of thorny bush, I headed down our hill to the big *soto* tree you and Clea call "Rocky." There I paused at my grave.

I've never told you about my gravestone. It's a piece of brown sandstone beneath Rocky. Using a wheelbarrow, I hauled it there last year. You might not even notice it since there are no words on the marker, only a small Miocene-epoch marine fossil from a time when an ocean covered all of Bolivia.

Sometimes when I pass it, I pause to remember my own bones becoming powder, my empty cranium grinning back at me. Yesterday, I ran a finger over my headstone's fossil. It's a sand dollar. Whenever I visit Lake Titicaca, I always taste that inland water body's salty water: another reminder. As you know, Titicaca is the last slurp of the ancient ocean. Even the soils our pod mixed in the minga contain deep-sea mineral traces.

During my graveside pause, I could hear the din from above: kids laughing and shovels striking hardpack. The air fragrant with eucalyptus, I took an acorn out of my pocket, one I brought back from Vermont, and placed it on my grave, knowing that the seed will never yield here since oaks need colder climes. As I stood beneath Rocky, a golden-billed saltator landed on one of the soto tree's low branches. These flamboyant birds frequent our land to feast on sunflowers. I gazed up at the saltator, and it cocked its black and orange head as if scrutinizing the acorn as a potential meal.

It's from saltators that I've been learning flexibility. Nothing fazes them. As our pants dry on the clothesline they've been building nests in the pockets. We took down those clothes, but the birds rebuilt two more times—in drying jeans' pockets—before they decided to try nesting elsewhere. (Unfortunately, in the hammock you love.) Finally, we constructed a few birdhouses. Clea painted them with pictures of flowers and seeds; now the saltators nest there.

Inflexible species can't survive. We humans must be nimble, adjust our thinking, and make quantum leaps in our empathy, creativity, and resourcefulness as we act—with a saltator's natural grit and calm—to face challenges that many see as impossible. I don't know what a saltator perceives, but I did wonder yesterday, as that bird abandoned the acorn and flew away over the *minga*, what it would take for humanity to see the rest of nature as our teacher. Every dolphin, every tree, every raindrop is alive in the life force, untainted by past regrets or future fears. Each saltator, butterfly, and flower opens up the way.

Some humans attracted to such teachings labor in *mingas* like ours in humble hillside towns, but they don't work alone. We ripple out together along frontiers of eco-villages and NGOs, Transition initiatives and organic farms, women's full-moon gatherings and workers' cooperatives, jailed elves and their everyday helpers, Malaysian living-bridge-braiders and Tennessee maverick sculptors. Our tiny pod contains millions.

Hi Daddy,

I miss the turtles! Tell Clea to give Shelby and Sheldon plenty of nispero. I miss you, Clea, and Melissa.
    "What are you going to **do** with your life?" *Everybody seems to be asking me that question. But isn't it one of those practical questions that is really a philosophical one? So I invented another way to ask it.*

Who are you going to **be** in life? In other words, will you be satisfied riding the fourth or fifth ring of somebody else's ripple, or will you journey inward and ripple out from there?

251

As I'm about to come celebrate with you guys in just one week, I imagine my quince a bubbling spring of yachachiywañu—a time to die and begin. The little girl Amaya dies and I become . . . what? I don't know. But I do know that I'm changing. I kind of feel like I'm at the top of a waterfall. I'm nervous and excited.

Dear Amaya,

Today, thinking back to your marvelous *quinceañera* celebration, my heart went back to the end of the evening.

Having helped cook and serve the feast, I felt exhausted. So exhausted, actually, that I didn't even have energy left for the traditional father-daughter dance. Plus, I knew you were itching, at that late hour, for the adults to leave you to your post-fiesta sleepover party in our living room.

But you insisted we dance. As Celia Cruz's "*La vida es un carnival*" kicked in, you reached out and pulled me out of my comfortable seat. Your friends looked a little surprised, but delighted, to see their amiga dancing "On 1" Cuban-style with her dad.

After the dance, the book of our letters-exchange burned in my hand. I wanted to finally give it to you.

But it wasn't the right moment. You were engaged with your friends.

It would have to wait for a picnic the following afternoon. Melissa and I followed you and Clea on a hike up to a parched rock outcrop below the pair of anonymous windswept hills high above our land that we've come to dub Clea Pampa and Amaya Pampa. I'd wrapped the hand-bound volume after tucking watercolors into the pages along with photos of us together as you grew up.

When I handed you your gift, you'll recall, you leafed through the pages thoughtfully, then hugged me, saying: "*Gracias*, Daddy." We lingered over our food, and the weather was perfect. No river, real or symbolic, flowed by. The outcrop we were on was surrounded by cacti and *agave* succulents; no metaphors or motifs grew there. Nor were any concepts or theories invited. The four of us talked and sometimes went silent. It was an ordinary moment, suffused with the life force. We chewed our food and gazed over the Samaipata Valley, our simple presence summing up the essence of your book gift.

Today in a text you told me you're working up a new ending to "Gaia's Seed," but you feel blocked. Writer's block, to me, is a bit like what happens when boulders landslide into streams. Water goes around these blocks, eroding them over time. I let such boulders be. You know those Chinese characters I inlaid in ceramic above my writing *casita* in our orchard? 自然, or Tzu Jan. Literally, it's "self ablaze," which to me is about the daily practice of seeing the ways I'm still programmed by Separation. But Tzu Jan is also the seed of Taoist poetry and philosophy, and it means: "occurrence appearing of itself." That is, things happen *through* us, but not *because of* us.

For example, as moons grew round, then skinny again, the letters I wrote to you completely changed. Autumn arrived with the yellowing of the pomegranate and soto leaves, then came a surprisingly frost-struck winter. Tzu Jan, all the while, kept pulling me back into the casita, and every day my hands wrote, painted, and *re*-wrote as Rocky the tree blazed below the orchard. Flocks of saltators rippled overhead, stream water gurgled blue, and grass crunched under turtles' wandering feet. As evenings fell over the mountain, the birds flaunted darkness as they darted east to bring the human realm rain.

Can language, and our imaginations, only be blocked by ourselves? If we allow words to stream as the rest of nature does, couldn't they emerge from us as lava flows, or some-times torrents, from volcanoes? I wonder. I do know that this dad's words clasp to realities like a daughter's warm hand. I remember how Clea took my hand and pulled me, one clear morning during your summer break, back toward you and Melissa.

At the time, I'd been opening our acequia to water a grove. Clea burst over and grabbed my hand. "Come quick," she cried, "It's *urgent!*" She dragged me, jogging all the way, to where you and Melissa were mixing soil in our tree nursery.

When I arrived, I asked, out of breath: "What is it? What's so urgent?"

Clea smiled. "But don't you know, Daddy? You have the *seeds.*"

We all laughed. Lots of things feel "urgent" to an eight-year-old who inhabits the present moment. I un-pocketed the persimmon seeds and handed them over.

You and Clea dug in, planting those seeds into loam alive with millions of microorganisms. Isn't it similar with Story? If you feel blocked—say, at your desk one drizzly Santa Cruz evening—while imagining your great-granddaughter, you might gaze out your window. Into the night rain.

The rains fall onto the Gihon and the Lamoille, onto the Piray and the unnamed creek through our land. They fall onto your persimmon seeds as they germinate, grow, and get graft-ed with initiation cuts. The rains will fall and the rivers will flow after everything we sense today has dissolved into humus for new seeds. And so there's time. Nevertheless, as your sister suggests—in millions of ways, wherever we live—how vital it is to seize the tools, prep the soil, and press seeds into future Gaia. Now.

Daddy!

I'm unblocked! So what happened was that I had a down day this morning, another stressed-out online class. To wipe away my negative feelings, I searched my mind for the positive and remembered what my art teacher told our class last week. It was so cool that I wrote it down: "The artist erodes worlds and channels time."

It got me inspired to begin again with future Gaia. First sentence: "Our Transition pod is small but contains millions . . . "

Like it?! The idea came to me under the mango tree where you and Mom baptized me. (Where you and I had our very first "conversation!" So it's fate??) Starting with your letter to me, I'll change names and details and turn them into future versions. Then Gaia will actually be a Powers like us! She'll be real because we'll use your real letter as the springboard. Then I'll use my diary for Gaia's thoughts.

First scene: Gaia is a teenager in another pod a hundred years from now, after another Covid—but there's no global warming and brain chipping and all that stuff. She lives in a world where you and me and everybody else today remembered her. So we're not going extinct in this future because my generation wakes up and learns to see through nature's eyes.

What do you think? Want to go there with me?

Rippling Further

Resources

To continue your journey beyond Separation and toward a healing reconnection with your own silent voice and the life force—in solitude and in tribe—here are some suggested resources.

The Watercourse

For reading groups using *Ripple*, <u>here are some prompting questions</u> on my website. To set up a virtual (or in-person, if possible) visit with your reading group, please <u>send me an email</u> at bill@williampowersbooks.com. For university classes using the book, I'm happy to engage with students in similar ways.

I facilitate a five-part "Water Course" which parallels the five portions of the journey we've traversed together from Aquifer to Ocean. This workshop channels *Ripple*'s practical, philosophical, and poetic currents into a transformative process for groups and individuals. The course is modular, and can be shaped to your group's needs, from short workshops through a full-semester format. You may <u>email me</u> for further information.

Topics

The resources arranged by topic below are also available in an expanded version on my website. (www.williampowersbooks. com) This online version is ever-evolving, since I integrate your suggestions through social media or email. The book *Ripple*, as well as Watercourse talks and my teaching above, draw from many of these resources:

Deep Ecology and Biocentrism

The Spell of the Sensuous by David Abram. Animal tracks, word magic, the speech of stones, the power of letters, and the taste of the wind all figure prominently in this intellectual tour de force that returns us to our senses and to the sensuous terrain that sustains us.

The Song of the World by Jean Giono. This tale of primitive love and vendetta is cast in a timeless landscape of river, mountain, and forest. The book gives a sense of a more biocentric world both through language and character.

Braiding Sweetgrass by Robin Wall Kimmerer examines deep ecology through the diverse lenses of personal memoir and scientific fact to argue for a new view of human involvement with the natural world.

The late theologian and ecologist Thomas Berry suggested that a deep understanding of the history and functioning of an evolving universe is a guide for our own effective functioning as individuals and as a species. Here are some videos of his talks. The wonderful Center for Ecozoic Studies shares Berry's "Great Work."

Meditation and Contemplative Practice

Ripple periodically surfaces the theme of our silent voice and "inner acre." How do we bring the interior space more consistently into the foreground in our daily lives? The future of Gaia (the imagined great-granddaughter; the planet) hinges on the cultivation of our inner world. Here are some ways to help cultivate it:

Ecotao and Quinta Conciencia are excellent, authentic meditation, natural healing, and experimental permaculture centers near Samaipata, Bolivia. Both are led by inspiring Bolivians who start with the cultivation of the inner world as the path to external change in regular retreats and workshops.

The Findhorn Community is an established ecovillage in Scotland where everyday life is guided by the inner voice of spirit and the voice of nature. The community's two hundred residents share a way of life in experiential workshops, conferences, and events which combine the ecological, spiritual, and "re-tribing" aspects discussed in *Ripple*.

Loving What Is, by Byron Katie. She shares "The Work" in this book, which is simply a process of remaining alert to and questioning stressful thoughts. It is a powerful and effective meditation practice I've used with my students. A worksheet and step-by-step process is available on Katie's website.

The Power of Now, by Eckhart Tolle. This guide's message is simple: living in the now is the truest path to happiness and enlightenment.

The New Story

<u>Living the Change</u> is a documentary that explores solutions to the global crises we face today—solutions any one of us can be part of—through the inspiring stories of people pioneering change in their own lives and in their communities in order to live in a sustainable and regenerative way.

The More Beautiful World Our Hearts Know Is Possible, by Charles Eisenstein. This thought-provoking book reminds us that we are all connected, and our small, personal choices bear unsuspected transformational power.

Active Hope, by Joanna Macy and Chris Johnstone. Navigates our choices to address the multiple crises that face us, and shows us how we need not be paralyzed but can indeed respond with resilience.

To get a sense of the New Story's opposite—the Story of Separation—here is <u>David Foster Wallace's full commencement speech</u> (audio) to the Kenyon College class of 2005. One listener writes of it: "Every time I feel I'm losing my way in life I come back to this speech."

Life Philosophy for Teens, College Students, and Beyond

The excellent films *Captain Fantastic* and *Leave No Trace* explore the intersection of youth, biocentrism, and coming of age.

On the Road by Jack Kerouac. More than the topic or plot, this book emanates a sense of freedom and possibility beyond Separation.

A Life of One's Own, by *Marion Milner*. How often do we ask ourselves, "What do I really want from life?" This classic book explores these questions as Milner embarks on a seven-year personal journey to discover what it is that makes her happy.

Remembering the Future and Speculative Fiction

David Fleming's *Surviving the Future* lays out a powerfully different new economics for a postgrowth world.

In an Ezra Klein Show podcast interview with Ted Chiang, the science fiction writer explores a range of topics from artificial intelligence, to animals, to the difference between magic and technology.

Jeff VanderMeer, the "weird Thoreau" who, through speculative fiction, grapples with our precious and fraught relationship with the natural world in his *Southern Reach Trilogy*.

Jaron Lanier looks at some of the big questions of our time through his books, including *Who Owns the Future?* along with *You are Not a Gadget*. He explores how we define and retain our humanity in the face of increasing artificial intelligence and social media.

In *Sapiens* and *Homo Deus*, Yuval Noah Harari looks through the macro lens of history so we can understand the only animal that can believe in an imagined order.

"Sorry to Bother You," a dark comedy written and directed by African American Boots Riley, in his directorial debut, that forces us to look at an "alternate" reality that may not be that far off.

Macrohistory

A Little History of the World by E.H. Gombrich tells the story of our species from the stone age to the atomic bomb. In between those epochs emerges a colorful sweep of our species' experience across the centuries.

Yuval Noah Harari's *Sapiens* (See "Remembering the Future and Speculative Fiction")

The Ascent of Humanity by Charles Eisenstein explores the history and potential future of civilization, tracing the converging crises of our age to the illusion of the separate self.

Simplicity and Minimalism

The first two books in William Powers' trilogy. *Twelve by Twelve* and *New Slow City*, are tales of intimate experiences with simplicity and minimalism, the first situated in rural North Carolina in an off-grid tiny house and the second in a similarly sized urban nest in New York City. Both books grapple with the personal philosophy and societal challenges to simplicity, and ultimately reveal the great joy and wisdom one can find in those beautiful parameters of "enough."

Your Money or Your Life, by Joe Dominguez and Vicki Robin, is a catalyst to transform your relationship with money. This illuminating book asks you some tough questions about guiding you to examine your earning, spending, debts, and savings.

Affluenza, by John DeGraaf, lays out how problems—ranging from loneliness, endless working hours, and family conflict, to rising debt, environmental pollution, and rampant commercialism—are all symptoms of a singular global plague: the incessant ambition for "more."

Be Self Sufficient-ish, by twins Andy and Dave Hamilton, is a practical guide on extracting oneself from the corporate economy and learning how to move towards self-sufficiency. They offer pragmatic and creative ways to live more thoughtfully and eco-friendly.

Ecovillages

The Global Ecovillage Network (GEN) was created to build bridges and catalyze the global relationships of communities focused on regenerative living. The network is made up of about ten thousand communities and related projects across cultures and continents where people are living together in greater ecological harmony.

The Amalurra Community was founded in a rural area outside Bilbao in the Basque Country of Spain and is one example of an ecovillage linked to GEN (see above), with 150 people living across three communities. Having sprung from the seeds of feminine principles, these communities balance ecology and spirituality with financial sustainability.

Tamera identifies itself as a peace, research, and education center, and is located in Portugal. It is a community of about two hundred people with a clear vision of decentralized and autonomous models of living for a postcapitalist world.

Dancing Rabbit Ecovillage is part of GEN and serves as an inspiring model of harmonious rural-community living in northeast Missouri, US. Founded in the 1990s in San Francisco, a group of eco-pioneers set out to model positive and sustainable living.

Tomorrow is a documentary about how to confront the multiple planetary crises in front of us with creativity and joy through real-life and concrete examples. It separates the issue into four key elements: agriculture, education, economy, and democracy.

Localism and New Economics

The Overspent American: Why We Want What We Don't Need by Juliet Schor, explores the social and cultural processes that drive individuals to spending and eventually into debt.

The Transition Network is a global movement of communities, born in the first "Transition Town" of Totnes, England. It includes over 1,500 towns and initiatives working towards the core principles of "Transition" with a key focus on eliminating the use of fossil fuels.

The documentary film "Transition 2.0" is a story of resilience and creativity that explores how we might get to a visionary future by taking steps now to avoid economic, energy and planetary catastrophe.

In Dispatches from the Sweet Life, William Powers tells the story of his family searching out balance, humanity, and happiness in a subtropical town in Bolivia, where the Andes meet the Amazon. Powers explores how his family's adopted town—Samaipata—was able to become a Transition Town, a model community that aims to increase self-sufficiency to reduce the potential effects of peak oil, climate destruction, and economic instability.

In a study in *The Solutions Journal* about Samaipata, Bolivia, research shows higher levels of happiness than countries that have per-capita income levels seventeen times higher. Moreover, the town's environmental impact is nearly seventeen times lighter than those same countries in the Global North.

Dying Well

The <u>Levine Talks</u> offer a wealth of wisdom from Stephen and Ondrea Levine, who over thirty-two years, provided emotional and spiritual support for those who are life threatened, and for caregivers through their Conscious Living/Conscious Dying Workshops. Near the end of Stephen's life, and from relative isolation in northern New Mexico, the couple offers deep reflection and moving anecdotes in candid conversation from their home.

<u>Memento Mori, or "Remember your Death,"</u> is the motto for one nun's initiative to get people to face death and be comfortable with it. In her forties, Sister Aletheia reaches a wide audience through social media platforms and offers online classes related to this project.

On the Shortness of Life, by Seneca, the Roman Stoic philosopher and playwright, offers a manifesto on how to get back control of your life and live it to the fullest. As Seneca reminds us:
It is not that we have a short time to live, but rather that we misuse a lot of the time we do have.

Permaculture, Organic Agriculture, and Bio-design

Inhabit is a documentary film exploring environmental issues facing us today and examining solutions that are being applied using the ecological design process called *permaculture*, a design lens that uses the principles found in ecosystems to help shift our impact from the destructive to the regenerative.

<u>The Permaculture Institute</u>, founded by Bill Mollison and Scott Pittman, brought the concepts of permaculture design to the Western Hemisphere from Mollison's home of Australia.

<u>World Wide Opportunities in Organic Farming</u>. Help out on a family organic farm during your next vacation, in exchange for room, board, and sustainability skills.

The Barefoot Architect, by Johan van Lengen, serves as a compendium of indigenous building techniques from across Latin America.

Animals and Humans

Daniel Quinn's provocative novel *Ishmael* takes us on a spiritual adventure to examine the hidden cultural—and speciesist—biases driving modern civilization.

<u>*The Cove*</u> is a wonderful 2009 American documentary film which analyzes and questions dolphin-hunting practices in Japan.

The documentary <u>*Food, Inc.*,</u> might just make you a vegetarian for life, once you learn the details of how mammoth corporations have taken over all aspects of the food chain in the United States, from the farms where our food is grown to the chain restaurants and supermarkets where it's sold.

Vandana Shiva, an eco-activist, agro-ecologist, and also known as an eco-feminist, is a modern-day revolutionary, and for forty years has been fighting a heroic battle on behalf of humanity and the ecologically besieged natural systems that support us. She has written twenty books and <u>*The Seeds of Vandana Shiva*</u>, a feature-length documentary, presents her remarkable life story.

<u>*The Superior Human*</u> is a documentary that systematically challenges the common human belief that humans are superior to other life forms. The film reveals the irrationality of this belief while exploring human bias.

Non-doing, Taoism, and Mindfulness

Lao Tzu's *Tao Te Ching* is referred to as not only the single most important text ever composed in China, it is probably the most influential spiritual text in human history. This recommended English translation shows how Lao Tzu's spirituality is structured around the generative life force and that this system of thought weaves the human into natural process at the deepest levels of being.

Ryōkan was a quiet and unconventional Sōtō Zen Buddhist monk in Japan who lived much of his life as a hermit. One collection of his poems, *Dewdrops on a Lotus Leaf*, beautifully reveals the whole range of human experience: joy and sadness, pleasure and pain, enlightenment and illusion, love and loneliness.

An Anthology of Classical Chinese Poetry, also translated by David Hinton, is a collection of the most important poems in the Chinese poetic tradition. The nearly five hundred poems provide a comprehensive account of the first three millennia of this rich tradition, with references to life, being human, and being with nature in ways that are strikingly relevant to our lives today.

How to Do Nothing, by artist and professor Jenny Odell, advocates for preserving our attention within an economy increasingly bent on commercializing it.

David Budbill's *While We Still Have Feet* pays homage to the long Chinese poetic tradition in his straightforward poems dispatched from his hermitage on Judevine Mountain in Vermont, US.

Art and Creativity

Amir Bar-Lev's film *Long Strange Trip* is a documentary film that reveals the essence of the band and its leader Jerry Garcia, who recognized and lived the principle of impermanence.

Lawrence Durrell's *The Alexandria Quartet* is a series of four books that take place in Alexandria, Egypt, before World War II. Pursewarden, a central character in the final book of the quartet, *Clea,* sums up the artist and artistic process as beautifully and aptly as anywhere.

Zen and the Art of Motorcycle Maintenance by Robert M. Pirsig uses the narrator's road trip with his son and two friends as a journey of inquiry into values.

The Vermont Studio Center has offered residencies to writers and visual artists since 1984 in its home of Johnson, Vermont. Based in a series of historic buildings overlooking the Gihon River in the northern Green Mountains, VSC provides studio residencies in an inclusive, international community, honoring creative work as the communication of spirit through form.

Race and Environmental Justice

Racial injustice—another form and effect of Separation—is being tackled now from an intersectional perspective that includes a focus on women's rights, climate change activism, and spirituality, with a sense of the trauma endured by generations.

Between the World and Me, by Ta-Nehisi Coates, offers a riveting perspective as a father speaks from personal experience to his son in urgent letters reckoning with our society and its relationship to race.

Black Faces, White Spaces by Carolyn Finney looks toward the future, highlighting the work of African Americans who are opening doors to greater participation in environmental concerns in the US.

In the award-winning documentary <u>Urban Roots</u>, a small group of dedicated citizens start an urban environmental movement with the potential to transform a city. With the most vacant lots in the country, Detroiters reclaim their spirits by growing food.

Media Literacy and Consumer Culture

<u>Adbusters Media Foundation</u> is an activist hub that publishes *Adbusters Magazine* with a creative mission to "smash ads, fight corruption, and speak truth to power." This is where memes like "Buy Nothing Day" and "Occupy Wall Street" got their start. Their <u>spoof ads</u> are poignant.

Maverick economist <u>Juliet Schor</u> analyzes the "Aquifer" level, researching trends in working time, consumerism, and the relationship between work and family. Her book *Born to Buy: The Commercialized Child and the New Consumer Culture* shows how advertising strategies convince kids that products are necessary to their social survival.

<u>The Campaign for a Commercial Free Childhood</u> is a network of experts, advocates, and forty thousand parents working to limit corporate marketers' incredible influence on kids' lives. They provide <u>these resources</u> and coordinate <u>Screen-Free Week</u>.

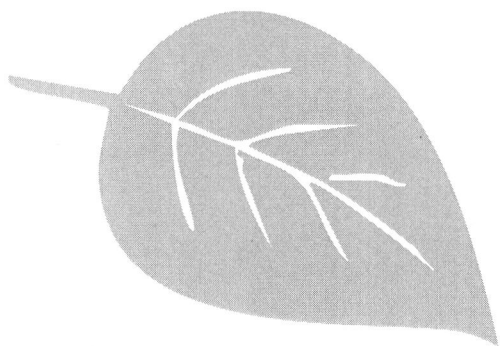